# ESSAYS ON
# HAYEK

FRIEDRICH A. HAYEK

Edited by Fritz Machlup
Foreword by Milton Friedman

# ESSAYS ON
# HAYEK

WILLIAM F. BUCKLEY, JR.
GOTTFRIED DIETZE
RONALD MAX HARTWELL
SHIRLEY ROBIN LETWIN
FRITZ MACHLUP
GEORGE C. ROCHE III
ARTHUR SHENFIELD

New York  *  New York University Press  *  1976

Library of Congress Catalog Card Number: 76-8360
ISBN: 0-8147-5409-0

Manufactured in the United States of America

# Notes on Contributors

**WILLIAM F. BUCKLEY, JR.** is the editor of *National Review* and a nationally-syndicated columnist. He has been host-adversary of the television show *Firing Line* for ten years, and is the author of 13 books. A 1950 graduate of Yale University, he first broke into prominence with the publication of his controversial *God and Man at Yale*. His most recent books are *Four Reforms; United Nations Journal* (based on his experiences as the United States delegate to the United Nations), and *Saving the Queen*, his first novel.

**GOTTFRIED DIETZE** is professor of political science at The Johns Hopkins University. He graduated from the law schools of the University of Heidelberg and the University of Virginia and received his Ph.D. degree from Princeton University. His books in English include: *The Federalist: A Classic on Federalism and Free Governments; In Defense of Property; Magna Carta and Property; America's Political Dilemma: From Limited to Unlimited Democracy; Youth, University and Democracy*, and *Two Concepts of the Rule of Law*. He is also the editor of *Essays on the American Constitution*.

**MILTON FRIEDMAN** received his M.A. degree from the University of Chicago in 1933 and his Ph.D. degree from Columbia University in 1946. He is Paul S. Russell Distinguished Service Professor of Economics at the University of Chicago, a member of the research staff of the National Bureau of Economic Research, and a contributing editor of *Newsweek* magazine. He is a past president of the American Economic Association and recipient of eight honorary doctor's degrees. He is the author of 19 books in English.

**RONALD MAX HARTWELL,** born in Australia, has been Reader in recent economic and social history at the University of Oxford since 1956, and recently visiting professor of economics at the University of Virginia. He was an editor of *The Economic History Review* from 1957 to 1972. His published works include: *The Industrial Revolution and Economic Growth; The Causes of the Industrial Revolution in England,* and *The Economic Development of Van Diemens Land, 1830-1850.*

**SHIRLEY ROBIN LETWIN** holds M.A. and Ph.D. degrees from the University of Chicago. While completing her doctorate, she studied under Professor Hayek. She has taught at the London School of Economics, Harvard, Brandeis, and the University of Chicago. Mrs. Letwin is the author of numerous essays, reviews, and two books: *Human Freedom* and *The Pursuit of Certainty: David Hume, Jeremy Bentham, J. S. Mill, Beatrice Webb.* She is completing a book on *A Modern Morality: Trollope's Gentleman.*

**FRITZ MACHLUP** received his doctor's degree from the University of Vienna in 1923. He came to the United States in 1933, where he has taught at several universities, including Harvard, Buffalo, Johns Hopkins, and Princeton. Since his retirement from Princeton, he has been professor of economics at New York University. He has served as president of the American Association of University Professors, the Southern Economic Association, the American Economic Association, and the International Economic Association. He holds six honorary doctor's degrees and is the author of 27 books in English.

**GEORGE C. ROCHE III** is president of Hillsdale College, an independent liberal arts college in Michigan. A native of Colorado, he received both his M.A. and Ph.D. degrees in history from the University of Colorado. He is the author of several books, including *The Balancing Act: Quota Hiring in Higher Education; Legacy of Freedom,* and *The Bewildered Society.* He was for five years director of seminars at the Foundation for Economic Education in Irvington-on-Hudson, New York. Dr. Roche is first vice president of the American Association of Presidents of Independent Colleges and Universities.

**ARTHUR SHENFIELD,** British economist and barrister, has served as a visiting professor at the University of Chicago and Temple University, and visiting distinguished professor at Rockford College, Illinois. He has been economic director of the Confederation of British Industry and director of the International Institute for Economic Research. Among other appointments, he has been economic adviser to the Government of Trinidad, chairman of the 1961-62 government commission on the cotton industry of Uganda, and chairman of the group of fiscal experts of the Business and Industry Commission of the Organization for Economic Co-operation and Development.

# Contents

# Notes from the Editor

This book is not designed as a *festschrift* nor as a volume of conference proceedings, though it shares some attributes of both: it is intended to honor Friedrich von Hayek and it contains essays presented at a conference. A genuine *festschrift* would have more contributors, most of them writing, not about the work of the man they wish to honor, but on a subject of their own choosing (though preferably in a field of interest to the honored person). Such a *festschrift* was, in fact, published under the title *Roads to Freedom*, edited by Erich Streissler *et al.* (London: Routledge & Kegan Paul, 1969, xix and 315 pages) with contributions by 14 of Hayek's friends and admirers. A genuine volume of proceedings would usually not be limited to the principal papers delivered at the conference; as a rule, it would contain also verbatim transcripts or condensed reports of the participants' contributions to the discussion of the papers. The present volume is confined to the major essays presented at a conference and to a foreword by the chairman of its opening session.

The conference at which the *Essays on Hayek* were delivered was a special regional meeting of the Mont Pelerin Society, held from August 24 to 28, 1975, at Hillsdale College in Hillsdale, Michigan. The editor believes that he should first enlighten those of the readers who do not know much, if anything, about the Mont Pelerin Society.

## The Mont Pelerin Society

This association was founded in April 1947. A group of 39 persons had been called together at the instigation of Friedrich von Hayek to exchange ideas about the nature of a free society, about the dangers to its survival, and about the ways and means of strengthening its intellectual support. The group included economists, philosophers, jurists, historians, political scientists, literary critics, and publicists. Some of them had known one another personally, some had been known only by their writings, but all were known as strong believers in political, economic, and moral freedom. They had come from ten different countries.

After spending ten days in intellectual communion on the beautiful Mont Pelerin, near Vevey, Switzerland, overlooking the Lake of Geneva, the group concluded that the discussions had been so stimulating and invigorating that opportunities for recurring meetings should be afforded by organizing a small international society of scholars, men of affairs, and men of letters (of both sexes, of course). The program of the society was clear, but the choice of a name was not. After rejecting a few proposed names, the group agreed to call itself, by the name of its first meeting place, the Mont Pelerin Society. The group adopted a concise "Statement of Aims," which well merits full reproduction at this point:

### STATEMENT OF AIMS

A group of economists, historians, philosophers and other students of public affairs from Europe and the United States met at Mont Pelerin, Switzerland, from April 1st to 10th, 1947, to discuss the crisis of our times. This group, being desirous of perpetuating its existence for promoting further intercourse and for inviting the collaboration of other like-minded persons, has agreed upon the following statement of aims.

The central values of civilisation are in danger. Over large stretches of the earth's surface the essential conditions of human dignity and freedom have already disappeared. In others they are under constant menace from the development of current tendencies of policy. The position of the individual and the voluntary group are progressively undermined by extensions of arbitrary power. Even that most precious possession of Western Man, freedom of thought and expression, is threatened by the spread of creeds which, claiming the privilege of tolerance when in the position of a minority, seek only to establish a position of power in which they can suppress and obliterate all views but their own.

The group holds that these developments have been fostered by the growth of a view of history which denies all absolute moral standards and by the growth of theories which question the desirability of the rule of law. It holds further that they have been fostered by a decline of belief in private property and the competitive market; for without the diffused power and initiative associated with these institutions it is difficult to imagine a society in which freedom may be effectively preserved.

Believing that what is essentially an ideological movement must be met by intellectual argument and the reassertion of valid ideals, the group, having made a preliminary exploration of the ground, is of the opinion that further study is desirable *inter alia* in regard to the following matters:

(1) The analysis and exploration of the nature of the present crisis so as to bring home to others its essential moral and economic origins.

(2) The redefinition of the functions of the state so as to distinguish more clearly between the totalitarian and the liberal order.

(3) Methods of re-establishing the rule of law and of assuring its development in such manner that individuals and groups are not in a position to encroach upon the freedom of others and private rights are not allowed to become a basis of predatory power.

(4) The possibility of establishing minimum standards by means not inimical to initiative and the functioning of the market.

(5) Methods of combating the misuse of history for the furtherance of creeds hostile to liberty.

(6) The problem of the creation of an international order conducive to the safeguarding of peace and liberty and permitting the establishment of harmonious international economic relations.

The group does not aspire to conduct propaganda. It seeks to establish no meticulous and hampering orthodoxy. It aligns itself with no particular party. Its object is solely, by facilitating the exchange of views among minds inspired by certain ideals and broad conceptions held in common, to contribute to the preservation and improvement of the free society.

*Mont Pelerin (Vaud), Switzerland, April 8, 1947*

Friedrich Hayek served for over 12 years as president of the Society and, when he resigned this office in 1960, was elected honorary president. Over the 29 years since its founding, the Society held 27 meetings in 12 countries: Austria, Belgium, France, Germany, Guatemala, Italy, Japan, the Netherlands, Switzerland, United Kingdom, the United States, and Venezuela. Faithful to its stated aims, the Society takes no actions, makes no public pronouncements, and does not engage in propaganda. Its only functions are to organize meetings to debate issues of public and international concern, and thus to afford its members, through exchanges of ideas with like-minded students of and believers in liberty, opportunities for recharging their moral batteries: these batteries are likely to run down or even go dead if their owners lack intellectual contacts with other analysts of the free society and are constantly exposed to the judgments of collectivists and "socialists of all parties."

All contributors to this book are members of the Mont Pelerin Society. Milton Friedman and Fritz Machlup are founding members (1947- ); Friedman served as president from 1970 to 1972, Machlup as treasurer from 1954 to 1959. Arthur Shenfield was president from 1972 to 1974. Gottfried Dietze has been a member since 1959, Ronald Max Hartwell and Shirley Letwin since 1969, George Roche since 1971, and William Buckley since 1972. Notes on the contributors are on pp. v-vii.

### Liberalism and Libertarianism

A strong attachment to liberalism unites the members of the Mont Pelerin Society, but it is the classical brand of liberalism, the one sometimes described as Nineteenth Century Liberalism, or liberalism in the continental European sense. Words have a habit of changing their meaning, especially if those who adopt them are not careful students of the literature or avid users of dictionaries. Thus it happened that, particularly in the United States, the word "liberalism" has been gradually appropriated by champions of collectivism who reject liberalism in its classical sense. (See my essay on "Liberalism and the Choice of Freedoms," in Erich Streissler, *et al.*, eds., *Roads to Freedom*, pp. 117-146.)

Old liberals may go on calling themselves by this designation—which is rightfully theirs—but they do so at the risk of being confused with American liberals. To avoid such confusion, they may resort either to explanatory footnotes or to adopting a new appellation for themselves, such as "libertarians." The most essential difference is that the classical liberal wants the individual to be free from coercive interferences, especially from interventions by the state, whereas the American liberal wants the state to intervene in all sorts of situations and restrict the individual's freedom of action in a variety of ways for a variety of objectives.

### Hayek, the Nobel Laureate

In October 1974 the Nobel Prize Committee announced that it had awarded the Nobel Prize in Economic Science to

Gunnar Myrdal and Friedrich von Hayek. The Mont Pelerin Society subsequently decided to celebrate this award to its founder and honorary president by devoting a regional meeting to a discussion of his work as scholar and teacher.

The editor does not believe that he should at this point provide either an appraisal or a biographical sketch of Professor Hayek. For such a sketch he may refer readers to the first section in his own essay—see pp. 13-14, below. For an official appraisal of Hayek he may be permitted to quote a few paragraphs from the Official Announcement of the Royal Academy of Sciences, republished by the *Swedish Journal of Economics*, Vol. 76 (December 1974), pp. 469 ff.; they refer in part also to Myrdal, with whom Hayek shared the prize, but the passages selected for reproduction here are those that relate chiefly to Hayek.

## Excerpts from the Official Announcement of the Royal Academy of Sciences

The Royal Swedish Academy of Sciences has awarded Professor Gunnar Myrdal and Professor Friedrich von Hayek the Prize in Economic Science in memory of Alfred Nobel for 1974. The Prize has been awarded for their pioneering work in the theory of money and economic fluctuations and for their penetrating analysis of the interdependence of economic, social and institutional phenomena.

The Academy of Sciences is of the opinion that, in addition to their contributions to economic theory, Myrdal and von Hayek have carried out important inter-disciplinary research so successfully that their combined contributions should be awarded the Prize for Economic Science.

Since the Economics Prize was inaugurated, the names of two economists, whose research has reached beyond pure economic science, have always been on the list of proposed prizewinners: Gunnar Myrdal and Friedrich von Hayek. They both began their research careers with significant works in the field of pure *economic* theory. In the main their early work—in the twenties and thirties—was in the same fields: theory of economic fluctuation and monetary theory. Since then both economists have widened their horizons to include broad aspects of social and institutional phenomena.

Mainly by directing most of his research to economic problems in the broadest sense, particularly the Negro problem in the USA and poverty in the developing countries, Myrdal has sought to relate economic analysis to social, demographic and institutional conditions. Von Hayek has extended his field of study to embrace such elements as the legal framework of economic systems and issues concerning the ways individuals, organizations and various social systems function. Both have been deeply interested in problems of economic policy and have therefore also studied changes in the organizational, institutional and legal conditions in our societies.

A quality which Myrdal and von Hayek have in common is a well-documented ability to find new and original ways of posing questions and presenting new ideas on causes and policies. This characteristic has often made them somewhat controversial. This is only natural when the field of research is extended to include factors and linkages which economists usually take for granted or neglect.

*** 

Von Hayek's contributions in the field of economic theory are both profound and original. His scientific books and articles in the twenties and thirties aroused widespread and lively debate. Particularly his theory of business cycles and his conception of the effects of monetary and credit policies attracted attention and evoked animated discussion. He tried to penetrate more deeply into the business-cycle mechanism than was usual at that time. Perhaps partly due to this more profound analysis, he was one of the few economists who warned about the possibility of a major economic crisis before the great crash came in the autumn of 1929. Von Hayek showed how monetary expansion accompanied by lending which exceeded the rate of voluntary saving could lead to a misallocation of resources, particularly affecting the structure of capital. This type of business cycle theory with links to monetary expansion has fundamental features in common with the postwar monetary discussion. The Academy is of the opinion that von Hayek's analysis of the functional efficiency of different economic systems is one of his most significant contributions to economic research in the broader sense. From the mid-thirties he embarked on penetrating studies of the problems of centralized planning. As in all areas where von Hayek has carried out research, he gave a profound historical exposé of the history of doctrines and opinions in this field. He presented new ideas with regard to basic difficulties in "socialist planning" and investigated the possibilities of achieving effective results through decentralized "market socialism" in various forms. His guiding principle when comparing various systems was to study how efficiently all the knowledge and information dispersed among individuals and enterprises is utilized. He concluded that only through far-reaching decentralization in a market system with competition and free price-fixing would it be possible to make full use of knowledge and information.

Von Hayek's ideas and his analysis of the efficiency of economic systems were published in a number of works during the forties and fifties and have without doubt provided significant impulses to the extensive and growing field of research in "comparative economic systems."

*Hayek's Responses*

This is a book on Hayek, not by Hayek. Of course, a scholarly appraisal of Hayek's work cannot refrain from providing many quotations. An ample supply of statements by him will therefore be found in the various essays that form the bulk of this book.

The proponents of this book were sorely tempted to include, for the reader's illumination, a reproduction of the Nobel Memorial Lecture which Hayek delivered in Stockholm, on December 11, 1974, under the title "The Pretence of Knowledge." This plan was discarded, because it would not be appropriate to include a major address by Hayek in a book designed to discuss and appraise his work. The lecture was published by the Nobel Foundation in the volume *Les Prix Nobel 1974* (Stockholm, 1975), pp. 249-258. It was republished as Part II of F. A. Hayek, *Full Employment at Any Price?*, Occasional Paper No. 45 of the Institute of Economic Affairs (London, July 1975).

It would not be inappropriate, however, to reproduce here the very brief speech which Hayek made at the banquet given to the Nobel Laureates in Stockholm after the presentation of the prizes. These few sentences, reprinted here with the kind permission of the Nobel Foundation from the volume *Les Prix Nobel 1974*, pp. 38-39, testify to Hayek's modesty and moral integrity:

*F. A. von Hayek*

Your Majesty, Your Royal Highnesses, Ladies and Gentlemen,

Now that the Nobel Memorial Prize for economic science has been created, one can only be profoundly grateful for having been selected as one of its joint recipients, and the economists certainly have every reason for being grateful to the Swedish Riksbank for regarding their subject as worthy of this high honour.

Yet I must confess that if I had been consulted whether to establish a Nobel Prize in economics, I should have decidedly advised against it.

One reason was that I feared that such a prize, as I believe is true of the activities of some of the great scientific foundations, would tend to accentuate the swings of scientific fashion.

This apprehension the selection committee has brilliantly refuted by awarding the prize to one whose views are as unfashionable as mine are.

I do not yet feel equally reassured concerning my second cause of apprehension.

It is that the Nobel Prize confers on an individual an authority which in economics no man ought to possess.

This does not matter in the natural sciences. Here the influence exercised by an individual is chiefly an influence on his fellow experts; and they will soon cut him down to size if he exceeds his competence.

But the influence of the economist that mainly matters is an influence over laymen: politicians, journalists, civil servants and the public generally.

There is no reason why a man who has made a distinctive contribution to economic science should be omnicompetent on all problems of society—as the press tends to treat him till in the end he may himself be persuaded to believe.

One is even made to feel it a public duty to pronounce on problems to which one may not have devoted special attention.

I am not sure that it is desirable to strengthen the influence of a few individual economists by such a ceremonial and eye-catching recognition of achievements, perhaps of the distant past.

I am therefore almost inclined to suggest that you require from your laureates an oath of humility, a sort of Hippocratic oath, never to exceed in public pronouncements the limits of their competence.

Or you ought at least, on conferring the prize, remind the recipient of the sage counsel of one of the great men in our subject, Alfred Marshall, who wrote:

"Students of social science must fear popular approval: Evil is with them when all men speak well of them."

## Acknowledgments

Before signing off and yielding to Milton Friedman for his Foreword, I should acknowledge my indebtedness to numerous people who have helped make this book possible or make it better than it would have been otherwise.

Let me thank first George C. Roche III, president of Hillsdale College, which hosted the conference at which the papers included in this book were presented. I thank the financial donors who made possible the Hillsdale meeting. Residual funds from that meeting have made this publication possible. For the permission to reprint the editor's essay on "Friedrich von Hayek's Contribution to Economics," and also the excerpts from the Official Announcement of the Royal Academy of Sciences, thanks are due to the *Swedish Journal of Economics*. For the permission to reprint Hayek's speech at the banquet in Stockholm, the kindness of the Nobel Foundation and of the Elsevier Scientific Publishing Company must be acknowledged.

In the preliminary editing of the manuscripts Timothy J. Wheeler and Eleanor McConnell were of great help, as was Jameson G. Campaigne, Jr. in advising on numerous technical aspects of the project. Vivian Lowe assisted in the design and layout of the book. Barbara J. Smith of Hillsdale College assisted in the proofreading. Nancy Henshaw retyped the manuscripts and assisted with the proofreading and with the preparation of the index. Malcolm Johnson, the director of New York University Press, and his able associates and assistants were most cooperative and deserve commendation. Last but not least, Don Lipsett, director of Foundation Relations, Hillsdale College, was the coordinator of the entire enterprise and kept all of us in line, including the officially responsible editor of this volume.

*FRITZ MACHLUP*
New York and Princeton
March 9, 1976

# Foreword

Friedrich Hayek's influence has been tremendous. His work is incorporated in the body of technical economic theory; has had a major influence on economic history, political philosophy and political science; has affected students of the law, of scientific methodology, and even of psychology. But from the particular perspective of the present book, all of these are secondary to Hayek's influence in strengthening the moral and intellectual support for a free society.

Over the years, I have again and again asked fellow believers in a free society how they managed to escape the contagion of their collectivist intellectual environment. No name has been mentioned more often as the source of enlightenment and understanding than Friedrich Hayek's. I cannot say that for myself, since I was influenced in this direction by my teachers at the University of Chicago before I had come to know Hayek or his work. But I, like the others, owe him a great debt. From the time I first read some of his works, and even more from the time in the mid-1940s that I first met Friedrich Hayek, his powerful mind, his moral courage, his lucid and always principled exposition have helped to broaden and deepen my understanding of the meaning and the requisites of a free society.

Like many others, I too, owe a great indirect debt to Hayek for the role he played in establishing the Mont Pelerin Society. I was fortunate enough to be in at the birth, at the founding meeting held in 1947 at Mont Pelerin, Switzerland. It was a great occasion, the bringing together on that mountaintop of a goodly company from all of the world, differing in many details, but all aware of the threat to freedom and all determined to do what they could, as intellectuals and as citizens, to stem and reverse the tide.

We cannot say that we have succeeded, but throughout the 28 years since its founding, the Mont Pelerin Society has veritably been a spiritual fountain of youth, to which we could all repair once a year or so to renew our spirits and faith among a growing company of fellow believers; the one time a year when a generally beleaguered minority could stop looking over their shoulders and let themselves go in a thoroughly supportive environment.

Hayek not only was the person most responsible for founding the Society; he was also the person more responsible than any other for its continued vitality and existence. It was therefore highly appropriate that a special regional meeting of the Mont Pelerin Society, held at Hillsdale College, Michigan, August 24-28, 1975, should be devoted entirely to various aspects of Hayek's work. Hayek himself, for understandable and commendable reasons, chose not to be present, but his beneficent spirit dominated the proceedings.

I am honored at being asked to write a brief introduction to this collection of the papers presented at that special meeting. The papers range widely, as they must to cover Hayek's contributions. George Roche, in a paper given at the opening session, sets the stage with a penetrating discussion of the implications of Hayek's work for the "moral and spiritual underpinnings of the free society." He stresses the importance of Hayek's "spontaneous order" for the formation of values as well as for the organization of economic activity and calls for a fusion of the many strands of thought—from libertarianism to traditional conservatism—that have animated believers in freedom. Fritz Machlup surveys Hayek's contributions to economics proper in his typical perceptive, encyclopedic, and lucid fashion. Arthur Shenfield introduces the reader elegantly to Hayek's forays into methodology, and into the source of some of the threats to freedom that have been generated by writings labelled "social science." Max Hartwell considers the role that historians have played in portraying a distorted picture of the achievements and problems of capitalism. That irrepressible Renaissance man, William F. Buckley, Jr., takes Hayek's famous polemic, *The Road to Serfdom*, as a starting point for an examination of the appeal of socialism to the intellectuals, not neglecting the contribution of businessmen to the undermining of a free society. Gottfried Dietze ranges over Hayek's contributions to the analysis of the political structure requisite to a free society, with special stress on Hayek's profound distinction between an imposed order and an order that develops without conscious intention out of the voluntary interaction of individuals. And as a final *pièce de résistance*, Shirley Letwin gives a subtle and sophisticated survey of the achievement of Hayek that managed to evoke perhaps a more spirited exchange of views than any other paper.

All in all, it was a true intellectual feast. Unfortunately, it has been possible to include only the main courses here. The side dishes and dessert, which added so much to the enjoyment of those of us who were fortunate enough to be present, consisted of the opening greetings by the current and immediate past presidents of the Mont Pelerin Society, Gaston Leduc and Arthur Shenfield, discussion of the main papers by panel members, comment and vigorous controversy from the floor, and remarks by chairmen of the several sessions. Many of these were of course not from prepared papers and it has been beyond the financial resources available to have them all transcribed, edited, and reviewed for publication.

The very least I can do, however, is to repeat here the program of main sessions so as to list the names of those persons who served as chairmen and formal discussants at the various sessions. I hope the readers will regard my rubbing in their loss in that way as offset by the acknowledgment which the participants so richly deserve for their contribution:

Opening Address:
**George C. Roche III:** *The Relevance of Friedrich A. Hayek*

Chairman: **Milton Friedman,** University of Chicago
**Fritz Machlup,** *Hayek's Contribution to Economics*
Discussants: **Fred R. Glahe,** University of Colorado
**Arthur Kemp,** Claremont Graduate School
**Gerald P. O'Driscoll, Jr.,** Iowa State University

Chairman: **Ralph Harris,** Institute of Economic Affairs
**Arthur Shenfield,** *Scientism and the Study of Society*
Discussants: **John A. Davenport,** Journalist and Lecturer
**Paul Gottfried,** Rockford College
**William N. Havender,** University of California, Berkeley

Chairman: **B. A. Rogge,** Wabash College
**Ronald Max Hartwell,** *Capitalism and the Historians*
Discussants: **Ole Jacob Hoff,** Author, Norway
**William H. Hutt,** University of Dallas
**Larry Wimmer,** Brigham Young University

Chairman: **John A. Howard,** Rockford College
**William F. Buckley Jr.,** *The Road to Serfdom:*
*The Intellectuals and Socialism*
Discussants: **Jean-Pierre Hamilius,** Esch/Alzette College, Luxembourg
**Henry Regnery,** Henry Regnery Company
**Stephen J. Tonsor,** University of Michigan

Chairman: **Alberto Benegas Lynch,**
Center for Studies on Liberty, Buenos Aires
**Gottfried Dietze,** *Hayek on the Rule of Law*
Discussants: **Danny J. Boggs,** Lawyer, Bowling Green, Kentucky
**Rhodes Boyson,** Member of Parliament, London
**Robert L. Cunningham,** University of San Francisco

Chairman: **Leonard E. Read,**
The Foundation for Economic Education
**Shirley Robin Letwin,** *The Achievement of Friedrich A. Hayek*
Discussants: **Manuel F. Ayau,** Francisco Marroquin University
**Israel M. Kirzner,** New York University
**Antonio Martino,** University of Rome

There is appended to the papers an appreciation of Hayek by
Authur Shenfield, and to Fritz Machlup's paper, a comprehensive bibliography of Hayek's scholarly publications.

I know I speak for all of the participants at the Hillsdale
meeting, as well as those who contributed in other ways to that
successful occasion, when I express the hope that this book will
help to spread to a still wider group Friedrich Hayek's influence
and example, especially to the young who are still forming their
philosophy, who would suffer the main consequences of the
loss of freedom, and who must play the major role in preventing
that outcome.

*MILTON FRIEDMAN*
Chicago, Illinois
February 11, 1976

George C. Roche III

# The Relevance of Friedrich A. Hayek

In the wake of winning the Nobel Prize in Economics, Professor Friedrich Hayek has received renewed attention from commentators throughout the western world. This widespread discussion of his work comes at a time when the mistaken assumptions of contemporary state interventionism and socialism have produced social, economic, and political deterioration on the grand scale. The clarity and perception of Hayek's world view are needed now as never before.

Friends of the free society have rejoiced in this fresh enthusiasm for Hayek's work. Always a key figure in the formulation of free market analysis, Professor Hayek has moved far beyond his early work in technical economics, expanding his horizons to include the whole spectrum of social theory. His analysis of the mistaken methodology which lies at the heart of scientism has made *The Counter-Revolution of Science* one of the important, though neglected, books of our times. His *Capitalism and the Historians* has played a major role in demythologizing the history of the Industrial Revolution. His *Road to Serfdom* threw down the gauntlet to the statists and social engineers at a time in the 1940s when the defenders of the free society were virtually without public influence.

Over the years the scope of the Hayek analysis has continued to grow. *The Constitution of Liberty* and, most recently, the initial volumes of *Law, Legislation and Liberty* have reflected a wide-ranging intelligence, building upon the premise of free market economics and gradually including all those elements of social, political, and philosophic concern which give vitality and validity to the free market idea.

Professor Hayek has come to believe that individual personality, together with the values, attitudes, and institutions which sustain that personality, form an inseparable portion of free market concerns. How men view themselves and their world finally governs the decisions of the marketplace; indeed, the values which men hold ultimately determine whether or not the market itself will be allowed to survive. As he phrased it in *The Constitution of Liberty*:

> In recent years valiant efforts have also been made to clear away the confusions which have long prevailed regarding the principles of the economic policy of a free society. I do not wish to underrate the clarification that has been achieved. Yet, though I still regard myself as mainly an economist, I have come to feel more and more that the answers to many of the pressing social questions of our time are to be found ultimately in the recognition of principles that lie outside the scope of technical economics or of any other single discipline. Though it was from an original concern with problems of economic policy that I started, I have been slowly led to the ambitious and perhaps presumptuous task of approaching them through a comprehensive restatement of the basic principles of a philosophy of freedom.[1]

Professor Hayek's work as a philosopher of freedom is badly needed just now. I need not convince you that the road ahead seems especially dark. Nor do I need elaborate upon the political difficulties, the intellectual barriers, which presently block return to the free society. Those obstacles are clearly formidable and they may well prove insurmountable. Yet we owe it to ourselves, and most certainly to our children, to explore the alternatives to serfdom and to lay the foundations for the moral and intellectual regeneration which the future may bring and which the continued existence of civilization so desperately requires.

Imperishably connected with this spirit of freedom and civilization have been the works of F. A. Hayek. In exploring Hayek's contributions to scientific knowledge and the free society, we are also exploring solutions to the overwhelming problems which we face today.

## The Present State of Western Society

As Hayek has pointed out again and again, there is no such thing as a control over the production of wealth which is not

---

[1] F. A. Hayek, *The Constitution of Liberty* (Chicago: University of Chicago Press, 1960), p. 3.

also a control over the lives of men. The enormous bureaucracy necessary for the "activist" state soon usurps the powers constitutionally allotted to the executive and legislative branches. The rule of law becomes a dead letter.

Such has been the process by which the freedom of the individual has been reduced in our time. No violent revolution; no armed dictatorship; everything appears in its usual form. Constitutions are still in force and democracy still functions, creating the illusion that all is well and that the people still rule.

But what a monstrous deception. Beneath the hollow forms of constitutional government grows an increasingly powerful state, manipulating democracy to serve its own ends and steadily reducing the area of individual self-determination.

There is little need to catalog the results: an all-encompassing welfare state, the ravages of inflation, the economic strangulation by state regulatory activity, and the interest-group politics which increasingly dominate the twentieth century. The result has been the politicized society, with all its attendant disasters for a freely working social order.

## Economic Science Is Not Enough

Advocates of the free market have consistently opposed the politicized society. The libertarian stance has gained strength over several decades as the failures of collectivism have mounted. The planning ideal, in both its European socialist and American liberal forms, has simply failed to function. The key point of libertarian attack has been the economic sector, since the failures of the collective ideal are most apparent and most easily measurable in that quarter. But as the western world casts about for a means of escape from the collectivist bog into which we have wandered, it is imperative that we remember, with Friedrich Hayek, that not all aspects of men and their institutions are measured within the realm of economics. The failures of collectivism strike at men's stomachs, but those same failures strike even more directly at men's souls.

There has been a tendency for libertarian economists to forget this fact, perhaps in an over-zealous attempt to apply scientific analysis to economic concerns. In his Nobel Prize acceptance speech on December 11, 1974, Hayek described the result of that entirely scientistic attitude within the field of economics:

> We have indeed at the moment little cause for pride: as a profession we have made a mess of things.
>
> * * *
>
> It seems to me that this failure of economists to guide policy more successfully is closely connected with their propensity to imitate as closely as possible the procedures of the brilliantly successful physical sciences—an attempt which in our subject may lead to outright error.[2]

In the conclusion of that same acceptance speech, Hayek reminded us:

> If man is not to do more harm than good in his efforts to improve the social order, he will have to learn that, in this, as in all other fields where essential complexity of an organised kind prevails, *he cannot acquire the full knowledge which would make mastery of the events possible.* He will therefore have to use what knowledge he can achieve, not to shape the results as the craftsman shapes his handiwork, but rather to cultivate a growth by providing the appropriate environment, as the gardener does for his plants.[3]

What is the "appropriate environment" to which Hayek refers? The depth and breadth of Hayek's scholarship should make clear the interrelation he has discovered between the economic sector and other portions of the social order. We cannot mend the damage of collectivist philosophy merely by discrediting economic interventionism. If we are to be effective in restoration of the free society, we must also address ourselves to the damage the collectivist ideal has done in other areas of men's lives. The working of a free economic order ultimately depends upon the moral and spiritual underpinnings of the free society as a whole.

It is in this area that collectivist philosophy has done the greatest damage. In fact, the public rejection of modern free market economics has not come about because the market fails to function, but because the collective ideal has distorted the institutional and moral fabric of society. Collectivism has

---

[2] F. A. Hayek, *Full Employment at Any Price?* (London: The Institute of Economic Affairs, 1975), p. 30.

[3] *Ibid.*, p. 42.

altered how men feel about themselves, their institutions, and their obligations, thus paving the way for the interventionist state. Until advocates of the free society are willing to carry on the argument on a level which reaches the individual and his moral concerns, which reinstates the certitudes and institutions around which men can order their lives and establish their identities, we cannot hope to turn the tide.

## The Moral Requirement

No society can function effectively for long without a deeply felt consensus on what it means to be a *good* man. The free society itself ultimately rests upon a particular conception of what the *good* man should be. Can the market function without respect for private property? Can individualism endure without respect for our fellow men, without regard for the rights of others? Can self-government exist divorced from what the American founding fathers called civic virtue?

The intensive interdependence of men within a society based upon the division of labor requires more than ever before the existence of a heartfelt moral consciousness. The free society is ultimately based upon the capacity of the individual to govern himself—from within. This capacity for self-government can and will break down if the proper moral climate does not exist. This is precisely what modern collectivism has done. It has eroded respect for all those things which hold a society together and which allow for peaceful social development. In a word, it has destroyed the ethics of the individual—his means to govern himself. By destroying the individual's only means for self-government from within, the perverted liberalism of our time has effectively destroyed the social matrix required by the free society.

A great many people today have lost their sense of purpose in life, their sense of spiritual direction and their sense of self-importance. They are without conviction. As C. S. Lewis would say, they are "men without chests." This loss of the spirit of true individualism poses a dire threat to the free society. Men who have thus lost themselves become ideal candidates for manipulation by others. They long for the crowd, demanding the "security" which the paternalistic state promises. Unable to discover the "unbought grace of life," people turn to materialism as the remedy. They find their happiness not in the love of friends, family and community, not in the drive for personal improvement, but in the spoiled child psychology—in sensual gratification and material things. Such remedies are never truly satisfying. The unquenchable thirst for greater satisfaction, for larger and larger doses of pleasure, impels such men into the arms of the state—which is more than happy to pose as generous benefactor and guardian. Government thus takes the place of family and community. It governs from without when the individual fails to govern from within. By this process it becomes totalitarian.

Like an individual, a society cut loose from its ethical moorings, contemptuous of its moral heritage, will not long remain free. As Burke said, its unbridled passion serves as the fire which forges its fetters. In fact, it may very well be that those who advocate the absolute freedom and autonomy of the atomistic individual are actually opposed to the basic conditions which make possible the free society.

The free society requires a competitive market economy. But it also requires an institutional and moral framework which provides the individual with his moral bearings, with a sense of freedom *and* responsibility. These elements, coupled with a properly limited government, constitute the preconditions for what Friedrich Hayek has described as the Rule of Law.

### A Working Definition of Freedom

Men must be free to choose and to act. But if this freedom is to be sustained, it must be guided by a moral awareness of the consequences of our actions upon those around us. In protecting the equality of all men under God and the law, society must be open, but not so open that the values which sustain men and which maintain civilization fall into decay. The elements of status, order, and tradition within the structure are not ends in themselves. They are means for the preservation of freedom and social cooperation. Society, as Mises insisted, is the means whereby we fulfill all our ends. If we destroy society through some misguided notion of pure individualism, we will find ourselves facing an individualism of the "noble savage" and the "trousered ape." There can be no freedom without a functioning social order. Freedom and order are both needed to hold society together. Social institutions are means for the preservation of peaceful human relations, serving as a governor on individual behavior. They preserve, in short, the Whig tradition which Professor Hayek has so brilliantly defended, preventing the spirit of freedom and civility from collapsing into anarchy.

Thanks, in large measure, to the insights of Professor Hayek, we now realize the intimate connection between freedom and social organization, between liberty and the Rule of Law.

## Conservatives, Liberals, and Libertarians

Professor Hayek may have shown us the way toward the free society. But much of contemporary discourse on the subject, even in conservative and libertarian circles, has shown us painfully unable to follow his lead. Perhaps at least a part of the problem lies in semantic confusion. In this confused age, not even our words have consistent meaning. Today such labels as liberal, conservative, and libertarian have so many definitions as to be almost meaningless. And yet these are the labels we have available to discuss our social order. With due apologies to all those liberals, conservatives, and libertarians who will insist that my definitions are inappropriate descriptions of their position, perhaps we should discuss for a moment what sort of political economy would be required to solve our present discontents.

The task that lies before us is of such a nature that neither atomistic libertarianism nor a mere conservatism of things past is sufficient for our purposes. As Professor Hayek has brilliantly pointed out, conservatism in this narrow sense lacks the knowledge of the economic underpinnings of civilization. Its devotion to tradition is frequently misplaced because it fails to see that all traditions themselves come from a *break* with some still older way of doing things. In addition, coerced tradition, like coerced innovation, is of little social value.

Order, like tradition, must originate within society and cannot be imposed from without.

Within the conservative framework, there has often been far too little room for freedom and innovation—for those impulses which keep society functioning. In fact, conservatism, at least in its narrowest sense, has tended to abhor change and extol the virtues of resignation and conformity with the status quo. Frequently such resignation to the past has been accompanied by a total rejection of scientific method as an appropriate tool of social analysis.

It may be objected that the "conservatism" I describe is a caricature of genuine conservatism. I myself am deeply attached to the necessity for tradition, and I harbor a healthy suspicion for the excesses of utopian rationalism. A loyalty to one's family, friends, institutions, and preferences is the very stuff of which real individualism and healthy societies are made. My point just now is simply that the negative, limiting side of what many people call "conservatism" provides an inadequate base on which to build a functioning social philosophy.

Neither will the philosophy of atomistic individualism fill our needs. This individualism was so short-lived in the nineteenth century because it contained the seeds of its own destruction, collapsing from within due to a defective core of values. Classical liberalism flourished in opposition to a repressive social structure. It functioned well in opposition to the status quo. When it gained ascendancy and had no more petrified social institutions to assault, when it became its own status quo, it turned inward to destroy itself. This is the history of the change from the classical liberalism of the nineteenth century to the collectivist liberalism of the twentieth century.

Liberalism was inseparably connected with science. It was the social philosophy of reason. But its chief difficulty consisted in its inability to keep scientific principles in their proper place. As one result, the "value free" position of economic science caused serious problems for the social structure. Liberalism has labored under great difficulty in understanding the difference between what is good for scientific analysis and what is good for men as members of society. From the position that science must, for the sake of objectivity, abstain from value judgments, the scientism of the twentieth century came to believe that values themselves are unscientific and—in an age of science—entirely unimportant. Soon the end seemed to justify the means. Values were thought to be "subjective" matters of personal preference. Anything that "worked" became good in and of itself. This is precisely the attitude which today threatens to bring civilization to its knees. Morality must be rooted, at least for the great mass of men, in something more deeply satisfying than utilitarianism.

Finally, there also was in classical liberalism an emphasis on the individual as an abstraction, as nothing more than an atomistic, interchangeable part in the social machine. This concept also stemmed from a failure to separate the realm of science from the realm of those values needed to sustain civilization. Methodological individualism—as Mises called it—is an invaluable tool of reasoning and economic analysis. But to some people, the concept came to mean that the individual is everything and that family and community are nothing. Atomistic individualism has proven pitifully incapable of forming a sound foundation for society. In thus rending the social fabric from within, it laid the groundwork for the rise of the collectivist state, paving the way for the very form of coercive social organization which classical liberalism most abhorred.

In saying these things, I do not question the value of science as such. I do not question its methodological principles, but I do maintain that what is good for the development of science is not necessarily good for the development of men, either as individuals or as members of society. Nor do I intend to criticize the fine intellectual efforts expended in the name of conservatism or classical liberalism or libertarianism. I do wish to suggest the shortcomings under which we have all labored, hopefully as a means of suggesting a broader and more effective future for the ideals of the free society.

## Spontaneous Order

Just now we need a new synthesis of those values and

insights which will allow us to restore the free society. In reaching that synthesis we must learn from our past mistakes and grasp the opportunity which the crisis of collectivism now offers us. To grasp that opportunity, we must offer workable alternatives to present discontents, workable alternatives in economic matters and social concerns. Nothing less will suffice. Here again, Friedrich Hayek's insights are a vital key.

One of Hayek's greatest discoveries and the keystone of his entire work on law and economics is the concept of "spontaneous order." This discovery, reaching back to Adam Smith and his analogy of the invisible hand, sees human society equipped with an internal gyroscope which produces spontaneous order: the market. The gyroscope organizes human activity without conscious, overall preplanning by a single man or any group of men and tends to provide a natural stability to society. Even when men supplant this natural or spontaneous order with some sort of planned society, the automatic workings of the market economy tend to reassert themselves. Though the internal gyroscope can be interfered with to varying degrees by government intervention, the market will move to correct itself the moment coercive force is removed, functioning to solve problems and produce social stability.

Hayek's analysis of spontaneous order has great potential to become a Golden Mean, a point of agreement among many differing views. It has the potential to offer solutions to modern liberals, while providing a basis for unity among the various factions of conservative and libertarian thought.

The principle of spontaneous order stands midway between the extremes of atomistic individualism and a totally planned social order. It disagrees with atomistic individualism by asserting that there are certain natural and essential bonds among men, bonds formed by the social matrix. But Hayek's spontaneous order also asserts the absolute necessity of personal liberty for the operation of any successful society. Standing midway between total change and the static society, spontaneous order suggests that there are institutional bonds which demand preservation, while still insisting that some change is both inevitable and desirable to meet with new conditions.

With regard to the divisions between conservatives and libertarians, the principle of spontaneous order agrees with the conservative emphasis on moral concerns and the preservation of a functioning social fabric. It asserts the necessity for an order in society, without imposing a planned order. Since traditions are developed over time, and necessarily without preplanning (that is, within the mode of spontaneous order), the Hayek idea reinforces the conservative respect for custom and the maintenance of viable tradition.

For the libertarians, spontaneous order enshrines personal liberty as the *sine qua non* of its operation. Hayek shows how any society, if it is to be a stable and lasting order, must be free. For Hayek, liberty is the necessary precondition for order, virtue and economic stability.

The principle of spontaneous order also has the potential to appeal to the modern day liberal. Many contemporary liberals, although disappointed with the results of the planned economy, nevertheless still agree with the announced goals of liberalism. They are seeking for an effective way to achieve human improvement, ensure the equitable distribution of wealth, protect the environment, and pursue similar humanitarian concerns. Looking at the results of the present-day interventions of government must indeed be a saddening experience for such contemporary liberals. The market principle is now receiving increasing attention from liberalism precisely because it ensures a regime of continuous reform and adjustment responsive to social needs. While avoiding the dangers inherent in utopianism, Hayek's spontaneous order has a demonstrated record of improvement for most of the western world, historically doing best for those on the bottom of the economic pyramid. Spontaneous order and the market idea have proven to be great problem solvers when allowed to function. The body of thought which is suggested by Hayek's concept of spontaneous order thus has direct validity to the concerns of our times, for sincere men of whatever persuasion within the western tradition. The work of Friedrich Hayek may well show us the way for the years immediately ahead.

Fritz Machlup

# Hayek's Contribution to Economics

This review of the scholarly publications of Friedrich A. von Hayek is arranged under the following headings: Biographical Sketch; Bibliographical Overview; Money, Credit, Capital, and Cycles; Socialism, Planning, and Competitive Capitalism; Legal and Political Philosophy; History of Ideas; An Essay in Psychology; Philosophy of Science; and Final Assessment.

## Biographical Sketch

Friedrich August von Hayek was born in Vienna on May 8, 1899 into a family of scientists and academic teachers. His grandfather was a biologist, specializing in zoology; his father, a doctor of medicine, turned to research in botany and lectured in this field as professor extraordinarius at the University of Vienna; one of F. A. Hayek's brothers became professor of anatomy at the University of Vienna; and his other brother, after a start in industrial chemistry, is now professor of chemistry at the University of Innsbruck. In view of this strong family allegiance to the natural sciences, F. A. Hayek's interest in economics, law, and philosophy seems to be an aberration. Such a hypothesis, however, would be mistaken in

Note: This essay was written in the summer of 1971 and published in *The Swedish Journal of Economics*, Volume 76, in December 1974 (pp. 498-531). The editors and publishers of the journal kindly gave me the permission to reproduce my essay in the present book, and I wish to acknowledge my indebtedness to them. Between 1971 and 1975 Hayek's bibliography has grown and I have attempted to bring it up to date. The biographical sketch—the first section of my essay—had been omitted in the *Swedish Journal* because the same issue contained the Official Announcement of the Royal Academy of Sciences, which included the essential biographical data of the Nobel laureate. I have now added a few sentences to the sketch, particularly those concerning the Nobel Prize and other awards received by Hayek since 1971.

as much as it fails to consider the maternal branch of Hayek's genealogy. His mother's father was professor of constitutional law and later statistician; he became president of the Central Statistical Commission of Imperial Austria. Still, the inclination toward the natural sciences in the family tradition was much stronger and has continued in the professional choices of Friedrich Hayek's children: his daughter is a biologist and his son a doctor of medicine doing research in pathology. It was probably inescapable that some of the writings of F. A. Hayek would touch on problems of the life sciences, especially biology and psychology.

Hayek's career as scholar and teacher has comprised an unusual amount of international migration: Vienna, London, Chicago, Freiburg, and Salzburg have been his "permanent" residences, apart from a good many places where he taught as visiting professor. He earned two doctorates at the University of Vienna—Dr. jur. in 1921 and Dr. rer. pol. in 1923—and became Privatdozent in Political Economy in 1929. From 1927 to 1931 he was director of the Austrian Institute for Economic Research. Early in 1931 he gave a series of guest lectures at the London School of Economics and, later in the same year, was appointed Tooke Professor of Economic Science and Statistics in the University of London. In 1944, London awarded him a D. Sc. degree; he also was elected Fellow of the British Academy. In 1950, Hayek accepted a position as Professor of Social and Moral Sciences and member of the Committee on Social Thought at the University of Chicago. His next move, in 1962, was to the University of Freiburg as Professor of Economic Policy. When he retired there in 1967, he accepted an appointment as honorary professor at the University of Salzburg, which awarded him an honorary doctor's degree in 1974. Apart from his activities in Austria, England, United States, and Germany, Hayek lectured in several countries on virtually all continents, most frequently in Japan, where Rikkyo University of Tokyo awarded him in 1964 an honorary doctor's degree. In 1971, the University of Vienna made him an honorary senator. In October 1974 the Swedish Academy of Sciences awarded him, together with Gunnar Myrdal, the Nobel Prize in Economics.

## Bibliographical Overview

A list of Hayek's scholarly publications from 1924 to 1973 is appended to this essay.[1] It is divided into four groups: books (B), pamphlets (P), books edited or introduced (E), and articles in learned journals or collections of essays (A).

Some of Hayek's 15 books appeared also in foreign translations. There are altogether 20 foreign-language editions (in eleven different languages), so that the combined count comes to 35 books. The bibliography contains 10 pamphlets, and 10 books edited or introduced by Hayek. This brings the number of items listed on file cards of library catalogues to 55.

The list of articles in learned journals or collections of original essays contains 131 titles. Of these, 83 are in English, 41 in German, and 7 in other languages. Reproductions or translations of articles in books of readings (anthologies) are not included in the list.

A classification by subject matter will be somewhat arbitrary since so many of Hayek's writings cover more than one field. I would assign five of his 15 books to (pure or monetary) economic theory, nine to political and legal philosophy and intellectual history, and one to psychology. Three of the books are collections of essays, most of them published previously. Of his ten pamphlets, four are on economic theory or policy, five on political philosophy, and one on a political issue. For his 131 articles I have attempted a more detailed breakdown:

| | |
|---|---|
| Economic theory | 45 |
|    Money and prices | 21 |
|    Capital and interest | 11 |
|    Investment cycles | 10 |
|    Growth and economic history | 3 |

---

[1] I have used, with some amplification of the references provided, the bibliography included in Erich Streissler, ed., *Roads to Freedom: Essays in Honour of Friedrich A. von Hayek*, London, 1969, pp. 309-315. Publications between 1969 and 1973 were added to the bibliography before the article published in the *Swedish Journal of Economics* went to the printer, and they were also included in the number count made for the text of this section. Later publications were listed as Addenda. It should be noted that this bibliography does not include articles in daily and weekly newspapers and in general-interest magazines.

### Money, Credit, Capital, and Cycles

My decision to discuss under one heading what some economists might treat separately is fully in conformance with Hayek's own view of these subjects. Additional money is usually issued by the way of credit to producers; credit gives them command over productive resources, which they use chiefly for the production of capital goods; and changes in the capital structure of the economy may take the form of cyclical sequences of booms, crises, and depressions.

At one point, after deploring that the theory of the trade cycle had not thus far received adequate assistance from the theory of capital, Hayek ventured the idea that in the future the relationship between the two theories may be reversed and that capital theory may benefit from the progress of cycle theory:

> Only by studying the changes of the capitalistic structure of production will we learn to understand the factors which govern it, and it seems that the trade cycle is the most important manifestation of these changes. It is therefore not surprising that the study of the problems of the trade cycle should lead to the study of the theory of capital (B-2, 2nd ed., p. 104).

Closely in line with this program, Hayek's first book was on *Monetary Theory and the Trade Cycle* (B-1, German ed. 1929); his second book, *Prices and Production* (B-2, 1931), explored the changes in capital structure due to the credit cycle; and, then, 32 articles and two books later, came his treatise on *The Pure Theory of Capital* (B-5, 1941).

*Early Steps: 1924–1931*

The first steps in this research program were a few articles published in German; the first two appeared in 1924 and

1925, after Hayek returned to Austria from a visit of the United States. The second of these articles was on "The Monetary Policy of the United States Since the Crisis of 1920" (A-2). He returned to the theme of the boom in the United States in another article in German (A-6, 1928, p. 67), in which he took exception to the view then dominant that the absence of rising price levels would guarantee lasting prosperity. He credited the slightly declining price level with the unusual duration of the prosperity but warned that a downturn might come as soon as the price level stopped declining. Perhaps I should remind the reader of the prevalent thinking of the time. The United States had reached a state of prosperity with an expansion of its monetary base, of its credit superstructure, of its investment and general business activity, but without an increase in its general price level. Economists almost unanimously praised this development, and some even announced that a "new era" had arrived with continuing prosperity without a danger of a subsequent crisis and depression. Hayek demurred: stability of the price level was not an assurance against a downturn; indeed it was covering up a large inflation of credit and an overexpansion of investment, which eventually would have to lead to a painful readjustment. In a comment which Hayek published in the Monthly Reports of the Austrian Institute for Economic Research (as its director) in February 1929, he boldly predicted that crisis and downturn in the United States might be imminent. With these warnings, which came true with a vengeance, Hayek had introduced one of the main theses of his monetary theory of the investment cycle.

Two other contributions to the subject of credit, capital, and cycles (A-7, 1928, and A-9, 1929) preceded the publication of his first book, all in German, and much noticed in Germany and Austria but not in English-speaking countries. Early in 1931, when Hayek was invited to give four lectures at the London School of Economics, which were published under the title *Prices and Production* (B-2, 1931), the "drama" began.

*The "Drama," 1931–1936*

It was Sir John Hicks[2] who referred to this period as a drama:

> When the definitive history of economic analysis during the nineteen thirties comes to be written, a leading character in the drama (it was quite a drama) will be Professor Hayek ... there was a time when the new theories of Hayek were the principal rival of the new theories of Keynes. Which was right, Keynes or Hayek?

Keynes' two volumes, *A Treatise on Money*, appeared in 1930, when Hayek's manuscript of *Prices and Production* was almost completed. Keynes, as editor of the *Economic Journal*, assigned Hayek's book to Piero Sraffa of Cambridge for review; Robbins, as editor of *Economica* assigned the Keynes work to Hayek for review. Hayek published his review article in two parts ("Reflections on the Pure Theory of Money of Mr. J. M. Keynes," A-10) in August 1931 and in February 1932. Keynes published a reply to Part I of Hayek's review (criticizing Hayek's book) in *Economica* in November 1931, and Hayek came back with a rejoinder in the same issue. Sraffa published his review article ("Dr. Hayek on Money and Capital") in March 1932. Hayek's reply to Sraffa appeared in June 1932 (A-12) together with Sraffa's rejoinder. These exchanges, however, were not the only ones. There were reviews, notes, and replies by Hawtrey, Pigou, and Robertson, to mention only those in the two journals edited in Cambridge and London. Of contributions in other journals we should mention the review by Arthur Marget in the *Journal of Political Economy*, April 1932, who compared the two rivals and sided with Hayek, and the article by Alvin Hansen and Herbert Tout ("Annual Survey of Business Cycle Theory: Investment and Saving in Business Cycle Theory") in *Econometrica*, April 1933, which incited a reply by Hayek ("Capital and Industrial Fluctuations," A-23) in April 1934.

In addition to his review of Keynes and his replies or rejoinders to Keynes, Sraffa, and Hansen and Tout, Hayek published between 1932 and 1936 ten articles on the subject, six of them in English. But after this sketch of the excitement

---

[2] Sir John Hicks, "The Hayek Story" in *Critical Essays in Monetary Theory*, Oxford, 1967, p. 203.

which Hayek's theories caused in those years, I must now turn to their contents.

### The Main Theses

The essential feature in Hayek's theory of the investment cycle is the "scarcity of capital," which in Spiethoff's theory had been the immediate cause of the crisis. Spiethoff's explanations, however, had never made it clear just how this scarcity came about and how it manifested itself. Hayek's model offered the elucidation how overinvestment would lead to scarcity of capital, compelling a cutback in investment and even the abandonment of some of the real capital that was produced owing to the excessive rate of investment.

For some of his most important theses Hayek gave generous credit to Knut Wicksell. Wicksell had seen that the controversy between the monetary and the structural theories of the business cycle was based on false distinctions since monetary causes could lead to structural disturbances. By lowering the market rate of interest below the natural rate—the rate of interest that would hold the rate of real investment down to the rate of voluntary saving—the banking system was able to initiate a cumulative movement away from equilibrium. Hayek made two important amendments to this thesis. First, the credit expansion need not be initiated by the banks lowering the money rate of interest; it could be initiated by a rise in the opportunities for profitable investment—for example, through a wave of entrepreneurial optimism or through technological inventions—which raised the natural rate of interest while the banks would satisfy the increased demand for credit at unchanged money rates (B-1, p. 95). Second, whereas Wicksell had assumed that equality of natural and money rates of interest would guarantee stability of the general price level and that, therefore, such stability would indicate that the banking system was lending at the natural rate, Hayek recognized (as, I believe, Myrdal had done independently) that stability of the price level and equality between investment and voluntary (or intended) saving may not be compatible with each other (B-2, 2nd ed., pp. 24ff.). In particular, in a growing economy the rate of interest that stabilizes the price level, by allowing a credit expansion corresponding to the increase in the volume of transactions, must be below the rate that keeps the supply of money capital at the level of voluntary saving (p. 27).

Hayek rejected three (at the time) generally accepted positions: (1) that money acts upon prices and production only if the general price level changes, (2) that a rising price level always causes an increase in production, and (3) that monetary theory was mainly, if not exclusively, the theory of how the value of money is determined. He demonstrated that almost any change in the quantity of money influences relative prices, no matter whether or not it changes the general price level; and that the real task of the theory of money is to show the influences of changes in the quantity and distribution of money upon the exchange ratios between different goods and upon the allocation of resources to the production of different goods. The most elementary distinction of this type is the distribution of monetary demand between consumers' goods and producers' goods (B-2, p. 36), but it is more useful to distinguish successive stages of production, from the earliest ones (those farthest away from consumption) to the latest stage, producing finished consumers' goods. Hayek showed what changes in the structure of production are ordinarily caused by changes in the proportion between consumer demand and investment demand (pp. 39-68).

Sudden changes in the proportions between consumer and investment demand, and thus in the structure of production, may lead to disturbances, and these disturbances are apt to take the form of crises if they involve a sudden need to shorten the investment period by requiring the use of more resources for the production of consumers' goods (p. 58). This need may arise either as a result of a sudden and drastic decrease in the supply of voluntary saving or as a result of a return to a normal rate of saving after an overexpansion of investment credits with the temporary "forced saving" that it involves. Drastic fluctuations of voluntary saving are not likely to occur with any frequency, but spells of forced saving are easily produced by the elasticity of bank credit, which reacts to an increase in demand by expansions of supply instead of increased market rates of interest. The induced increase in investment causes a lengthening of the production process or, in a more modern terminology, a deepening of the capital structure. The new structure could be maintained only if the new proportion between consumer demand and investment demand could be maintained. Since the additional money funds paid out to the factors of production employed in increased proportions in the earlier stages of production are almost certainly, with only brief time lags, going to swell the demand for consumers' goods, the artificially achieved new proportion can be maintained only if investment funds are continually increased by bank credit (and dishoarding) supplied at a continually increasing rate. This, however, cannot happen, either because the banks find it impossible or too risky to go on expanding at an increasing rate (p. 90), or because investors find it too risky to go on borrowing and investing. As soon as the inevitable increase in consumer demand becomes large enough to increase the proportion of consumer to investment demand, productive factors will be shifted away from earlier stages of production. It will prove impossible to complete some of the longer production processes; particular producers of capital goods will find it unprofitable to continue producing at full scale; other stages of production will be affected by the slow-down; and capital invested there will lose in value, and some may even have to be abandoned.

This exposition of the cyclical sequence of induced lengthening and painful reshortening of the capitalistic production process under the influence of changes in the proportions of monetary demand is then supplemented by Hayek's exposition of the same sequence in terms of relative prices. He advances a most ingenious theory of the price structure that induces firms to make the reallocations of resources leading to the described changes in the capital structure. He constructs a model of the price mechanism that accomplishes first the shift of non-specific resources from later to earlier stages of production, then their retransfer to later stages, and he shows a behavior of profit margins in line with these adjustments, inclusive of the appearance of heavy losses in those early stages that use, but will be unable to use fully, specific real capital such as buildings or machinery not adaptable to other uses. Hayek's innovation consists in making changes in the rate of interest equivalent to changes in the price margins obtainable by producers in different stages of production. If the entire margin between prices of original factors of production—let us think of wages of labor—and prices of finished consumers' goods is interpreted as interest for the time elapsed between the input of factors and the output of consumption goods, and if the whole production process is subdivided into stages the number of which increases when the process is lengthened and decreases when it is shortened, then the margin obtained by each stage will decline when the process is lengthened and increase when the process is shortened (pp. 74-78, 91). A reduction in the rate of interest will be the equivalent of a narrowing of price margins, and an increase in the rate will be the equivalent of their widening. The widening of the margins indicates that only the "less capitalistic" (shorter) production processes can be profitable, while the "more capitalistic" (longer) ones lose money and some of them are abandoned, leaving specific capital goods partly or fully unused, and complementary nonspecific factors of production unemployed.

The inevitability of the crisis attending the adjustment of the economy after its overextension, a crisis resulting in excess capacity of durable capital equipment and in unemployment of labor, is probably the most characteristic (and most criticized) thesis in Hayek's theory of the trade cycle. Since in his model the crisis begins when consumer demand reasserts itself (after having been suppressed in real terms by the artificial enlargement of credit-financed investment), the possibility of avoiding or curing the depression through even greater support to effective demand is questioned, if not definitely denied, by Hayek (A-23; B-2, p. 154). The policy implication of his theory is that support to investment demand would be wrong, since overextension of credit and investment was the basic disease; but support to consumer demand would also be wrong, since it was its increase that

stopped the investment boom and forced the painful adjustment; to increase it even more would induce a shortening of
the production period far beyond what is called for by
normal saving and consumption habits. The recipe, therefore,
was to let the depression run its course (p. 99). Hayek
recognized the possibility of a "secondary" deflation of credit
and demand, which might theoretically be avoided by the
right monetary policy, but he saw no possibility of ascertain-
ing in practice where the necessary adjustment ended and the
"secondary monetary complications" began.

### Supplementary Theses

The fundamental thesis of Hayek's theory of the business
cycle was that *monetary* factors *cause* the cycle but *real*
phenomena *constitute* it (B-2, 2nd ed., p. xiii). Several hypotheses about the monetary factors must therefore supplement
the main thesis concerning the real phenomena.

The most interesting of the supplementary hypotheses are
those that pertain to the construct of "neutral money,"
another idea that goes back to Knut Wicksell (B-2, p. 31). By
Hayek's definition, money is neutral if all exchange ratios
among goods and services are what they would be if money
did not exist except as a *numéraire* in a general-equilibrium
system; that is to say, therefore, if they are not affected by
the existence of money as a means of payment and store of
value.

Hayek made it clear that this was only a pure construct, an
instrument of analysis, but not a precept of policy, even if we
might be well advised to establish a monetary system and
pursue a monetary policy that would approach the condition
of neutrality. A stable price level in a growing economy
would surely not satisfy this condition, and a rising price level
still less. A constant quantity of money would come closer to
it were it not for changes in the velocity of its circulation and
in the coefficient of money transactions (which measures the
money work to be done in relation to given volumes of
production, which is altered when, as in the case of a merger
between a supplier and his chief customer, payments of
money are replaced by mere bookkeeping operations). Not

only would it be practically very difficult to adjust the quantity of money for just these variations in its effectiveness but, as Hayek fully realizes, the additional requirements of neutrality, that all prices are completely flexible and all contracts are based on correct anticipations of future price changes, are too far from actual conditions to make neutral money a possible goal of policy.

Apart from these discussions of an ideal money system, Hayek presents some sharp insights into the system as it actually works. Some of his strictures against the "elastic system" that our monetary authorities try to manage with a view to keeping interest rates stable, and especially to keep them from rising, have not lost their timeliness. Indeed, some of the ideas which Hayek shows to be fallacious have gained in strength since the 1930s; a re-reading of Hayek's theses on stabilizing monetary policies might have a beneficial influence on the policy makers of the 1970s.

## *A Methodological Note on Aggregative Theorizing*

I was especially cheered by a brief methodological remark of Hayek's on the differences in approach between monetary and general economic theory. I hope my readers will understand my desire to call their attention to it.

Hayek finds it intellectually unsatisfactory

> ... if we try to establish *direct* causal connections between the *total* quantity of money, the *general level* of all prices and, perhaps also the *total* amount of production. For none of these magnitudes *as such* ever exerts an influence on the decisions of individuals: yet it is on the assumptions of a knowledge of the decisions of individuals that the main propositions of non-monetary economic theory are based.... If ... monetary theory still attempts to establish causal relations between aggregates or general averages, ... [it] lags behind the development of economics in general. In fact, neither aggregates nor averages do act upon one another ... (B-2, 2nd ed., p. 4).

With this remark Hayek anticipated a discussion which many years later engaged the protagonists of macro-economic and micro-economic analyses and which established, at least to my satisfaction, that we have not completed our task before we have ascertained the micro-economic basis of all macro-economic theorizing. If an authority is to be cited in support of this proposition, I choose Robert Solow.

## Ideas Have Their History

In proposing new hypotheses some eminent writers are prone to refer to previous literature only in order to show how wrong all or most of their predecessors had been and how great an advance in knowledge their own work therefore constitutes. Hayek, in sharp contrast with this practice, goes out of his way to find and show all traces of the ideas he offers for our consideration. As an enthusiastic but honest historian of ideas, he presents us with careful miniature histories on virtually every major issue that figures in the development of his theories. At least one reviewer—Arthur Marget (*J.P.E., loc. cit.,* pp. 262 and 263)—pays tribute to "the fine feeling which Dr. Hayek shows in the way of scholarly appreciation of the achievements" of past theorists and to Hayek's modest and "calm scholarship" in contrast with the "swinging and assured brilliance" of some of his rivals.

Examples of such miniature histories of ideas are the doctrinal surveys of theories of money and prices, creation of bank credit, forced saving, and neutral money, to mention only a few of those presented in connection with Hayek's first two books.

## The Rivalry with Keynes

Hayek's review articles of Keynes' *Treatise* (A-10, 1931 and 1932) angered Keynes' constituency in Cambridge and left them with the feeling that Hayek had misunderstood and misinterpreted their master's theories. I suspect, indeed I confidently believe, that the most loyal followers of Keynesian views, if they now re-read Hayek's criticisms, would accept many of them partly or fully. Keynes himself probably did so after he had progressed from the *Treatise* (1930) to the *General Theory* (1936), in which he repudiated many of his previous propositions and formulations.

I want to refer particularly to Hayek's critique of Keynes' views on Saving and Investment (A-10, Part I, p. 24). Keynes either had never read or had seriously misunderstood Wicksell's exposition. His constructs of $S$ and $I$ were quite different from Wicksell's, yet he came to the very same conclusion which Hayek and Myrdal had found erroneous in Wicksell's argument, namely, that the rate of interest that would equate $S$ and $I$ would also keep the general price level stable.

Good Keynesians would also accept Hayek's critique (*loc. cit.*, p. 40) of the explanation of the trade cycle in Keynes' *Treatise*. Keynes, at that time, thought that increases in prices of consumers' goods and in the resulting profits (windfalls) were the principal criteria of the boom. Needless to say, an increase in investments was part of Keynes' 1930 model of the boom, but it did not play the major role that it was correctly assigned in the 1936 model presented in the *General Theory*. There are many other points on which Hayek's critical comments were well taken but which at the time added to the antagonistic feelings in the rival camp.

With the appearance of the *General Theory* the "drama" was ended. By then, after several years of the Great Depression, it had become clear that Hayek's prescription of "waiting it out" was inopportune. Only few students of the depression were willing to give earnest consideration to hypotheses from which so unacceptable policy recommendations were derived. In those years of "secular" stagnation and unemployment, a model for which full employment was the starting assumption could not compete with one that was based on underemployment equilibrium and from which a prescription of vigorous government action for more employment was derived. Keynes' new theory of underinvestment and underconsumption was victorious, not only over Hayek's theory of overinvestment and overconsumption but also, for a period of years, over all economic analysis that featured micro-economic equilibria and optimal resource allocation at a time when general unemployment of virtually all kinds of resources was the prevalent condition almost everywhere.

## Scholars' Appreciation of Hayek's Hypotheses

The victory of Keynes' theory on the political scene and in the halls of the universities did not mean that all scholars turned their backs on Hayek's hypotheses. I want to present the testimonies of four eminent economists who recognized the validity of the Hayekian models of the maladjusted time-structure of production.

Sir Dennis Robertson, though unwilling to accept Hayek's hypotheses as a general theory of the trade cycle, found them valid as a description of special kinds of cycles and fully applicable as explanation of some of the industrial fluctuations in the nineteenth and early twentieth centuries. As an illustration he pointed to the crisis of 1909 with the preceding boom and the subsequent depression.

Joseph Schumpeter took a similar position.[3] Let him speak for himself:

> ...the reader knows by now that the author is not a wholesale admirer of Professor von Hayek's theory *as far as it claims to be a fundamental explanation* of the causes of the cycle. All the more it is a duty to point out that the course of American events in the twenties and thirties of the nineteenth, not less than the course of events of the twenties and thirties of the twentieth century, invites interpretation in terms of that theory. In fact, when we observe the behavior of the price level which was such as to negative all idea of "inflation" according to one definition, and the behavior of the banking sphere which spells violent inflation according to another definition, and when thereupon we further observe what happened between 1836 and 1840, fairness almost compels us to tender to that eminent economist our most sincere congratulations.

Again, with regard to the 1850s, Schumpeter recognized (*op. cit.*, p. 333) "the presence of a Hayek effect: in a very obvious sense the period of production was lengthened beyond what the economic organism could stand for the moment."

Sir John Hicks (*op. cit.*, pp. 210 ff.) appreciated Hayek's model as a contribution to the theory of growth:

> The Hayek theory is not a theory of the credit cycle. . . . It is an analysis—a very interesting analysis—of the adjustment of an economy to changes in the rate of genuine saving. In that direction it does make a real contribution. But it is a contribution which, when it was made, was out of due time. It does not belong to the theory of fluctuations, which was the centre of economists' atten-

---

[3]Joseph A. Schumpeter, *Business Cycles*, Vol. 1, New York and London, 1939, p. 296 n.

tion in 1930; it is a fore-runner of the growth theory of more recent years.

According to Hicks, some of the issues to which Hayek drew attention were such "that economists found it hard to understand and which perhaps even now [1967] have not been completely cleared up" (*op. cit.*, p. 203). The Hayek theory may apply to the inflationary conditions of our time, for if "rapid" inflation

> is to be kept down to a finite rate of inflation, there must be unemployment. This is the Hayek "slump." To such conditions the Keynesian prescription is irrelevant, as irrelevant as Hayek's was in 1931. Hayek's prescription—the direction of policy towards the restoration of the marginal productivity of labour to a normal level . . . —will then after all be right (p. 215).

Erich Streissler (*op. cit.*, pp. 245 ff.) agrees with Hicks that the major use of the Hayek model is in the theories of long-term economic growth. He regards Hayek's studies on the durability of capital goods his "most important and permanent contribution" to the theory of capital (p. 259), and he points to places, periods, and sectors of the economy to which the "Hayek process" applies—presumably not only as explanation of rates of growth but also as explanation of cyclical phenomena. He emphasizes the building industry (p. 272), the inventory cycle (p. 275), and the formation of human capital through investment in education (p. 283):

> Thus Hayek's theory of capital in its most full-scale development finds its most fruitful application today in the analysis of the problems of qualified labour, of the economics of education. In human capital we find all the features of the Hayek process.

He mentions the trend toward lengthening the investment period, interrupted by a process of shortening it when job opportunities become particularly favorable.

*Elaboration and Reconstruction of Capital Theory*

When his ideas, which first had "fascinated the academic world of economists"[4] got "out of fashion," Hayek did not give up; he continued to elaborate, refine and reformulate his theories. Some of this work is included in his fourth book, a collection of essays under the title *Profits, Interest, and In-*

---

[4]Nicholas Kaldor, "Professor Hayek and the Concertina-Effect," *Economica*, November 1942, p. 359.

*vestment* (B-4, 1939). The main theme was to show "why under certain conditions . . . an increase in the demand for consumers' goods will tend to decrease rather than to increase the demand for investment goods" (p. 3). He explained how the "principle of acceleration of derived demand" could become inverted into a "deceleration principle" (p. 33).

The collection contains also an article on "The Maintenance of Capital" (A-27), to which a reply by Pigou and a rejoinder by Hayek were published in 1941 (A-43). These and other studies can be regarded as part of Hayek's work for a reconstruction of capital theory. His *Pure Theory of Capital* (B-5, 1941) was, to my knowledge, the first full treatise on capital since Böhm-Bawerk's *Positive Theory* and Irving Fisher's two volumes on interest theory. (Wicksell's analysis was part of more general economic studies.)

Hayek's *Pure Theory* appeared at a time when writers and teachers of economics were concerned with problems of unemployment, war finance, rationing, industrial organization, and government control of business; they had no time and no inclination to concentrate on some of the most complex and difficult abstractions regarding a subject that did not seem to have any direct relevance to the "real" problems of the day. Indeed, most textbooks that appeared during and after World War II simply omitted the parts or chapters on capital theory that had been regarded as indispensable in earlier times and are now once more considered indispensable in the training of economists. Thus, Hayek's *Pure Theory* failed to excite or fascinate the economists as his writings had done ten years before. It is, however, my sincere conviction that this work contains some of the most penetrating thoughts on the subject that have ever been published.

I shall confine myself to listing a few of the themes to which this book has made most significant contributions. Hayek's construct of "intertemporal equilibrium" is presented in a refined form (pp. 22-25), as is his model of the interest rate as a ratio between the prices of the factors of production and the expected prices of their products in relation to the time interval between purchasing the former and selling the latter (p. 38). The problem of the "physical productivity of

investment" is elucidated with remarkable clarity; the increase
in the stream of outputs from given inputs in processes that
require longer periods of investment is attributed to the combination of the inputs "with forces which could not be put to
any use during the shorter period" (p. 72). The phenomena of
natural growth and fermentation, and the use of materials,
tools, and accessories are described as a "vertical or successive
division of labor" (p. 73).

The "period of investment" is analyzed for the four cases
of "point input–point output," "continuous input–point output," "point input–continuous output," and "continuous input–continuous output" (pp. 67-69). The concept of an
"average period of production" is replaced by that of a
spectrum of different investment periods which are "incom-
mensurable in purely technical terms" (p. 145). On this point
I may, however, recall Wicksell's dictum that we ought to
retain the concept as a "general principle" of heuristic value
even if it is "without direct physical or psychic significance"
(*Lectures*, Vol. I, p. 184). Hayek rejects also the concept of a
"supply of capital" except as a complete enumeration of "all
the alternative income streams between which the existence of
a certain stock of non-permanent resources (together with the
expected flow of input) enables us to choose" (p. 147).
Nevertheless, after introducing the notion of the "force of
interest" (in continuous compounding), Hayek arrives at an
equilibrium position in which all rates of increase in all
individual processes of production are equalized, exhibiting a
determinate "marginal productivity of an investment" (p.
179). I mention only one more issue: that of "durable goods,"
where Hayek shows that equalization of marginal products com-
prises the choice between varying the durability of any individual good and varying the number of goods of given durability
(p. 214).

In selecting the themes for this enumeration I have followed my preferences as a teacher; others might have chosen
different issues as the most noteworthy. As far as subsequent
studies by other authors are concerned, I find most of them
disappointing, partly because of their failure to proceed from
where Hayek left off or to reconsider what may be in need of

revision. An exception is the monograph by Robert Solow, which has added valuable insights and clarifications of these vexing problems.[5]

## Capital and Interest Revisited

Hayek never regarded his work as definitive. On at least two occasions he returned to problems of capital and interest: he reconsidered the relative roles of productivity and preference and he elucidated what he called the Ricardo Effect.

If the rate of interest is the rental paid for loanable funds, determined by supply and demand; if the net supply of such funds is ultimately determined by saving and, hence, by preferences of decision-makers regarding present and postponed consumption; if the demand for such funds is ultimately determined by investing and, hence, by the considerations of decision-makers regarding the productivity of using present inputs for the production of future outputs; and if the rate of interest, as observed over the years, is not drastically different over time but varies only within relatively narrow limits; should one attribute this relative stability to a property of the productivity functions or to a property of the preference functions? This question was answered differently in the literature: for example, Irving Fisher, Frank A. Fetter, and Ludwig von Mises placed major emphasis on preference; whereas Knut Wicksell and Frank M. Knight stressed productivity.

Hayek tackled this question at least four times, first in a German article (A-5, 1927), later in a much more deeply probing article in English (A-32, 1936); afterwards in his *Pure Theory of Capital* (B-5, 1941); and once again in a brief note in English (A-56, 1945). He first sided with those who gave the predominant role to the productivity function and reached the following conclusion (A-32, p. 53):

> While the process of saving still continues, the rate of interest will be determined solely by the productivity of investment . . . and the psychical attitude will merely determine how much will have to be saved at every moment in order that the marginal rate of time-preference may adapt itself to the given and constant productivity rate.

---

[5] Robert Solow, *Capital Theory and the Rate of Return*, Amsterdam, 1963.

The chief reason for this conclusion was that, for shorter income periods, "the indifference curve becomes more and more curved, while the transformation curve remains unchanged" (p. 56). Since, "compared with time-preference, the productivity of investment will always be comparatively constant," the latter exerts a stabilizing influence on the rate of interest (p. 55).

Hayek retracted this conclusion in 1945 (A-56), because it applies only to the case of an "evenly progressive economy" and did not take account of regressive movements, "when the supply of capital decreases" or "falls short of the amount in the expectation of which previous investments have been made" (p. 24). In such a case there may be a movement along the productivity curve where it has a sharp bend—that is, where it is no longer a nearly straight line or only slightly concave—and there "time-preference takes charge" (p. 25). The new conclusion is that

> so long as "time-preference" remains constant or falls, the productivity element will be dominant; but whenever "time-preference" rises, it takes control and we may get as a result sudden and violent increases in the marginal productivity of investment, and, in consequence, of the rate of interest.

The other revisited problem is that of the Ricardo Effect, first treated under that name in the essay that gave the title to his fourth book (B-4, 1939). Hayek later explained that, after Schumpeter and others had spoken of the "Hayek Effect," he wanted to disclaim originality and to point to its real originator by renaming it "Ricardo Effect." (Some critics, however, especially Kaldor, *op. cit.*, p. 364, have questioned Hayek's interpretation of Ricardo's proposition.) Hayek came back to the problem in a chapter of his *Pure Theory* and in an article published in 1942 (A-45), where he provided a revised exposition. Then, 27 years later, reacting chiefly to an interpretation by Hicks (which Hayek considered to be in error), Hayek published "Three Elucidations of the Ricardo Effect" (A-127, 1969).

The original proposition by Ricardo said that a rise in wages will encourage capitalists to substitute machinery for labor, and a fall in wages will make them substitute labor for capital. If real wages are seen as the ratio of factor prices to product prices, one can interpret a rise in product prices as a fall in factor prices. Hence, a rise in the prices of final output will, like a fall in wages, lead to the substitution of labor for capital, that is, a decline of investment in early stages of production.

This theme called for elucidation and Hayek provided it. To those who continue to hold that an increase in consumers' demand must raise the demand for investment goods, he said (pp. 284-285):

> If it were true that an increase in the demand for consumer goods *always* leads to an increase in investment, even in a state of full employment, the consequence would be that the more urgently consumer goods are demanded the more their supply would fall off. . . . The mechanism which prevents such a result is the Ricardo Effect. And though its operation may not be obvious for a long time because of the more apparent monetary complications, and may even be altogether suspended as long as there is general unemployment, sooner or later it must reassert itself.

### Socialism, Planning, and Competitive Capitalism

Under this heading I propose to survey Hayek's writings on socialism, capitalism, planning, free markets, competition, and economic policy insofar as their focus is on economic analysis. In a subsequent section I shall survey partly the same and partly other writings on economic systems and social institutions insofar as they focus on legal and political philosophy. This separation may occasionally do some violence to Hayek's argument but is justified from the point of view of the autonomy of the disciplines (though Gunnar Myrdal may object to that notion). Hayek explained his great interest in moral, legal, and political philosophy as that of

> an economist who discovered that if he was to draw from his technical knowledge conclusions relevant to the public issues of our time, he had to make up his mind on many questions to which economics did not supply an answer. (From the Preface to *Studies in Philosophy, Politics, and Economics,* B-13, 1967, p. vii.)

Nevertheless, since we do not in this survey have to pass judgment on the desirability of public policies and institutions, we may try to separate contributions to technical economic analysis from clarification of the philosophical background that is required for moral judgment and political advice.

*Economic Calculation for Socialist Planning*

The problem of the possibility of rational economic calculations in planning under socialism had been raised and formulated by Ludwig von Mises in 1920, further elaborated in 1922, and defended against critics in 1924 and 1928. Hayek edited in 1935 two volumes on the subject: one entitled *Collectivist Economic Planning* (E-5) with essays by several authors, the other on *Economic Planning in Soviet Russia* by Boris Brutzkus (E-6). To the latter he contributed a preface, to the former two essays. In 1940, he published an article (A-41), chiefly to review books in which Oskar Lange and Henry D. Dickinson presented "solutions" to the problem. Hayek later included his two essays and the article as chapters 7, 8 and 9 in his collection *Individualism and Economic Order* (B-7, 1948).

In the first of these essays, on "Socialist Calculation: The Nature and History of the Problem," Hayek gave a scholarly history and pre-history of the idea. He found some seeds in the writings of Hermann Gossen, Edwin Cannan, and Georg Sulzer, and some seedlings in the writings of Nicolaas G. Pierson, Enrico Barone, and Otto Neurath.

The second essay, "Socialist Calculation: The State of the Debate," went beyond the task which Hayek set himself in its title in that he added new issues to those already debated. The most important thought, the fact that "given" knowledge—of capacities, technologies, tastes—is not "concentrated anywhere in a single head" and not readily available for use "in the calculations of the central authority" (E-5, p. 155), appears here for the first time. (In later years Hayek made this thought the central theme of other publications.) Hayek distinguished the problems of assembling the data, setting up the equations, working out the results, making the decisions, and conveying them to those who have to execute them. He showed that to sacrifice the freedom of consumer's choice would simplify the problem but would not make it soluble as long as somebody's aims or preferences, say, that of a dictator, are to be satisfied "with any degree of rationality or consistency" (*op. cit.*, p. 160). Anticipating Lange's "competitive solution," Hayek remarked that "only if competition exists not only *between* but also *within* the different industries can we expect it to serve its purpose" (p. 171). However, he conceded that the "impossibility" of finding a solution could not be proved and he expressed the hope that, "now that the world is moving in that direction," a rational system of resource allocation under socialism would be found after all (p. 180).

Hayek distinguishes five positions of socialist writers on the issue in question: (1) a nonposition, the original Marxian scorn for any attempt to go beyond the analysis of the laws of motion under capitalism and to anticipate what evolution might bring; (2) the position that consumers' preferences need not be obeyed and, therefore, that there is no problem about values, prices and costs; (3) the position that socialism should dispense with calculations in terms of value and calculate instead in terms of natural, physical units such as energy; (4) the position that calculation in terms of prices was indeed necessary, but their determination by market competition could be replaced by mathematical techniques with which the planning authorities would determine all values and quantities by means of a general-equilibrium model; and (5) the position that prices of consumer goods and of labor could be determined through competition in markets, all other prices fixed by a board in such a way that supply and demand are equated, and all quantities be decided by production managers committed to produce as cheaply as possible and to equate marginal costs to the fixed prices.

This last position is examined by Hayek in his "Socialist Calculation: The Competitive 'Solution' " (A-41 and B-7, Ch. 9). Hayek had anticipated in his second essay much of what Lange in 1938 and Dickinson in 1939 proposed, but now that these proposals were on the table he could probe their practicality as well as their internal consistency. Much of what Hayek had to say about the difficulties that would complicate or frustrate the operation of the proposed "market socialism" has in later years been learned by experience and observed in practice by leaders of economic reform movements in Hungary, Czechoslovakia, and Poland. The problems which Hayek found insoluble are still unsolved, and the makeshifts which he judged to be inferior or unworkable are still in an admittedly unsatisfactory state. The accepted aim is decentralization of decision-making, but the questions of costing, pricing, responsibility, risk-taking, incentives, testing for success and failure, investment decisions, and all the rest are still waiting for any more acceptable answers than Hayek considered possible.

In his final appraisal of the plans for market socialism Hayek expresses the fear (B-7, p. 208) that the proposed schemes

> are so thoroughly unorthodox from a socialist point of view that one rather wonders whether their authors have not retained too little of the traditional trappings of socialist argument to make their proposals acceptable to socialists who are not economists.

Twenty-eight years after these words were published, a group of dedicated socialists trying to decentralize the system and make it more liberal, more productive, and more humane, learned to their distress, shared by most of the intellectual world, that Hayek's fears had been justified.

## Planning, Competition, and the Use of Knowledge

One of the most original and most important ideas advanced by Hayek is the role of the "division of knowledge" in economic society. He devoted to this problem two articles (A-34, 1937, and A-55, 1945), both of which are included in his 1948 volume of essays (B-7, Chs. 2 and 4). I shall use direct quotation rather than paraphrase to bring out the major points:

> The really central problem of economics as a social science ... is how the spontaneous interaction of a number of people, each possessing only bits of knowledge, brings about a state of affairs ... which could be brought about by deliberate direction only by somebody who possessed the combined knowledge of all these individuals (B-7, p. 51). How can the combination of fragments of knowledge existing in different minds bring about results which, if they were to be brought about deliberately, would require a knowledge on the part of the directing mind which no single mind can possess? (p. 54.) Planning in the specific sense in which the term is used in contemporary controversy necessarily means central planning—direction of the whole economic system according to one unified plan. Competition, on the other hand, means decentralized planning by many separate persons.... Which of these systems is likely to be more efficient depends mainly on the question under which of them we can expect that fuller use will be made of the existing knowledge. This, in turn, depends on

whether we are more likely to succeed in putting at the disposal of a single central authority all the knowledge which ought to be used but which is initially dispersed among many different individuals, or in conveying to the individuals such additional knowledge as they need in order to enable them to dovetail their plans with those of others (p. 79).

What matters in this connection is not scientific knowledge but the unorganized "knowledge of the particular circumstances of time and place"; practically every individual "possesses unique information of which beneficial use might be made" (p. 80), but which "cannot be conveyed to any central authority in statistical form.... Central planning ... cannot take direct account of these circumstances of time and place" and "decisions depending on them" must be "left to the 'man on the spot' " (p. 83). "We need decentralization because only thus can we insure that the knowledge of the particular circumstances ... will be promptly used" (p. 84).

"Fundamentally, in a system in which the knowledge of the relevant facts is dispersed among many people, prices can act to co-ordinate the separate actions of different people ..." (p. 85). The price system is "a mechanism for communicating information" and "the most significant fact about this system is the economy of knowledge with which it operates" (p. 86). The problem is not that a unique solution *could* be derived from a complete set of "data," but that "we must show how a solution is produced by the interaction of people each of whom possesses only partial knowledge" (p. 91).

## Competition and Free Enterprise

In two papers first published in the collection of essays (B-7, Chs. 5 and 6) Hayek examines the role of competition in a capitalist economy. He criticizes modern micro-economic theory, especially the theories of the firm and of the industry, for their preoccupation with static analysis of models of pure and perfect competition and for their scant attention to competition as a dynamic process (p. 94).

For Hayek the important problem lies in attempts "to discover new ways of doing things better than they have been done before" (p. 101); "the argument in favor of competition does not rest on the conditions that would exist if it were perfect" (p. 104). For the social benefits from competition are unimportant; what matters are instances "where competition is deliberately suppressed" (p. 105).

Those who know Hayek as a dedicated "libertarian" may be surprised about his condemnation of a tradition which held that "with the recognition of the principles of private property and freedom of contract ... all the issues were settled, as if the law of property and contracts were given once and for all in its final and most appropriate form, i.e., in the form which will make the market economy work at its best" (p. 111). Hayek has harsh things to say about the uses of the freedom of contract by which the "competitive order" is transformed into its opposite, "ordered competition" (p. 111). He seriously questions "the extension of the concept of property to such rights and privileges as patents for inventions, copyright, trade-marks, and the like" (pp. 113-114). Similarly, he questions the extension of "the freedom of the individual ... to organized groups of individuals" and the extension of "the rights of a natural person" to "corporations as fictitious or legal persons" (p. 116). In all these matters the present legal framework may be inappropriate to the objective of making competition more effective.

In subsequent years Hayek devoted more analysis to these problems. With the problem of the corporation, its rights, powers, and economic consequences, he dealt in two articles (A-71, 1951, and A-98, 1960). The problem of trade unions, their rights, powers, and economic consequences, was the subject of two articles (A-84, 1958, and A-91, 1959) as well as a significant chapter in his work on *The Constitution of Liberty* (B-12, 1960, Ch. 18). A special subject, taxation, especially for redistributive purposes, was treated in papers (A-73, 1952, and A-79, 1956) and in a chapter of the volume just mentioned (B-12, Ch. 20). This large volume contains also chapters on social security, the monetary framework, housing and town planning, agriculture and natural resources, and education and research. Because these chapters were part of a work on legal and political philosophy they have not received much attention from economists.

## Legal and Political Philosophy

In one of his many philosophical papers—on "Kinds of Rationalism" (A-112, 1965, p. 9)—Hayek feels compelled to explain why he, "at one time a very pure and narrow economic theorist, was led from technical economics into all kinds of questions usually regarded as philosophical." He tells that he was searching for more adequate

> insight into the relations between the abstract rules which the individual follows in his actions, and the abstract overall order which is formed as a result of his responding to the concrete particular circumstances which he encounters, within the limits imposed upon him by those abstract rules. It was only through a re-examination of the age-old concept of freedom under the law ... and of the problems of the philosophy of law which this raises, that I have reached what now seems to me a tolerably clear picture of the nature of the spontaneous order of which liberal economists have so long been talking.

In order to comprehend better how "the man-made rules and the spontaneous forces of society interact," we need "a much closer collaboration between the specialists in economics, law, and social philosophy than we have had . . . ."

Hayek's writings on legal and political philosophy account for a substantial share in the number of his publications. Nevertheless, the present review of his work is predominantly concerned with Hayek the economist and will therefore be confined to little more than a selective listing, and occasionally the academic reception, of his contributions to the philosophy of law and politics.

### Freedom and the Economic System

Hayek's first publication directed to this subject, under the title I have chosen for this subsection, was a pamphlet published in 1939 (P-2). It was followed by a brief note in *Nature* (A-44, 1941), addressed chiefly to natural scientists. Then came the book that became a bestseller in many countries, *The Road to Serfdom* (B-6, 1944). It was published in three English editions and translated into ten foreign languages. It aroused heated discussions, was lavishly praised and roundly panned by the critics according to their own political stance; and the prediction of one reviewer, Joseph J. Spengler, came true: that "Hayek's views will probably be distorted by

Right and Left."[6] I should like to quote from the reviews of a small sample of respected economists.

A. C. Pigou called it "a scholarly and sincere book"[7] and believed that few scholars will "close the book without a feeling of respect for and sympathy with the writer."[8] Aaron Director held that "economists should be grateful to Professor Hayek" for his explorations of "the ultimate political implications of abandoning the competitive system. There is no economist writing in English more eminently qualified to do this job."[9] Joseph Schumpeter called it

> a courageous book: sincerity that scorns camouflage and never minces matters is its outstanding feature from beginning to end. Finally, it is also a polite book that hardly ever attributes to opponents anything beyond intellectual error.

With regard to the concluding chapters of the book, Schumpeter expects that the "reader will be glad to have the views of one of the most eminent economists of our time."[10]

## Liberty and the Law

*The Road to Serfdom* did not satisfy Hayek's scholarly standards. He submerged himself into the study of social, political, and legal philosophy, and provisional fruits of this effort became available in the form of articles and essays (A-74, 1953; A-78, 1955; A-87 and 88, 1958; A-89, 92, and 93, 1959) and a small book with the title *The Political Ideal of the Rule of Law* (B-11, 1955). All this was preparatory to a volume which some of Hayek's admirers regard as his chef-d'oeuvre, *The Constitution of Liberty* (B-12, 1960, x and 570 pages).

Some of the chapters on economic institutions and policies have been mentioned before; the parts concerned with philosophical problems and jurisprudence remain to be described, but even this we shall suppress in favor of quoting from a

---

[6] *Southern Economic Journal*, Vol. 12, 1945, p. 51.

[7] *The Economic Journal*, Vol. 54, 1944, p. 217.

[8] *Ibid.*, p. 219.

[9] *The American Economic Review*, Vol. 35, 1945, pp. 173-174.

[10] *Journal of Political Economy*, Vol. 54, 1946, p. 269.

review article by Lord Robbins,[11] so that we can get an appraisal from an eminent economist and historian of ideas:

> The recognition of an order in society which has not been planned as a totality is clearly fundamental; and never has the pathbreaking significance of the great eighteenth century discoveries in this respect been better set forth than in Professor Hayek's luminous exposition, itself the source of many new insights. As he develops the conception of a spontaneous organization which is not only a sorting out of comparative aptitudes and technical advantages, but also a means of utilizing and developing a heritage of knowledge never capable of being grasped as a whole by any of the participants in the process, the time-honoured theme of the advantages of the division of labour assumes a new aspect; and propositions that have been repeated more or less parrot-wise for a hundred and fifty years acquire a meaning and depth seldom before realized. I would venture to pick this out, together with his earlier papers on similar topics, as one of Professor Hayek's most enduring contributions to our subject.

Robbins concludes with a vote of gratitude and admiration, "gratitude for a splendid contribution to the great debate, admiration for the moral ardour and intellectual power which inspired it and made it possible."

This great work done, Hayek did not rest. He could not let go of a topic on which he found so much more to do. In an article in German (A-100, 1961) he asks why it is that personal liberty is in continual jeopardy and why the trend is toward its being increasingly restricted. The cause of liberty, he finds, rests on our awareness that our knowledge is inevitably limited. The purpose of liberty is to afford us an opportunity to obtain something unforeseeable; since it cannot be known what use individuals will make of their freedom, it is all the more important to grant freedom to everybody (p. 103). Liberty can endure only if it is defended not just when it is recognized to be useful in particular instances but rather continuously as a fundamental principle which may not be breached for the sake of any definite advantages obtainable at the cost of its suspension (p. 105). It is not easy to convince the masses that they should sacrifice foreseeable benefits for unforeseeable ones.

This piece was followed by a number of small ones, some

---

[11] "Hayek on Liberty," *Economica*, February 1961, pp. 66-81. The quotations are from pp. 69-70 and 81.

in German (A-105 and A-106, 1963; A-111,1965; and A-120, 1967), some in English (A-114, 1966; A-115, 1967; and A-121 and A-123, 1968), in which Hayek added many new nuances to his ideas, and several novel thoughts on liberty and the legal and social order. In "The Principles of a Liberal Social Order" (A-115) Hayek made some useful semantic remarks about the difference between liberalism and democracy (and their opposites, totalitarianism and authoritarianism), the former indicating the extent, the latter the site of governmental power. Of interest is the idea of defining an economy as a decision-making unit, and thus to deny this designation to the totality or "catallaxy" of independent individual "economies" in a community or nation; socialism transforms a catallaxy into an economy. In the same article he proposes that "the basic principles of a liberal society may be summed up by saying that in such a society all coercive functions of government must be guided by the overruling importance of what I like to call *the three great negatives: peace, justice,* and *liberty*."

In "The Constitution of a Liberal State" (A-121, 1967) Hayek offers ideas for radical changes in the separation of powers in democratic society. He attributes the influence of pressure groups favoring the interests of particular groups or individuals to the fact that the same legislative assembly has both the power of making general laws and the power of directing the government in providing services of all sorts. "A legislative assembly confined to the articulation of universally applicable rules of just conduct whose effects on particular individuals or groups would be unforeseeable, would not be under such pressure." Hayek, therefore, proposes "two distinct representative assemblies," charged with altogether different tasks. I must resist the temptation of mentioning, let alone discussing, the numerous ways of democratic reform proposed by Hayek.

### History of Ideas

Hayek is recognized as one of the most scholarly, most erudite, and most interesting historians of ideas in economics as well as in legal, political, and social philosophy. His list of publications in this area includes 24 articles and essays on individual writers; five or six comprehensive surveys of schools of thought and intellectual movements; one book (on *John Stuart Mill and Harriet Taylor*); and five books by major economists which he edited or introduced; in addition, several of his topical books contain large chunks that are devoted to presentations of the history of the ideas with which Hayek is concerned at the moment. I have briefly commented on this in connection with Hayek's work on the theories of money, capital, and the trade cycle.

*Men's Lives, Works, and Thoughts*

On some of the great writers of the past Hayek wrote complete biographies with careful discussions of their works and seminal thoughts. On some he prepared obituaries, but even these are much more scholarly than what ordinarily goes under that name. With regard to others, Hayek was not concerned with either their lives or their complete works but only with particular ideas of theirs. Finally, there are some very important authors whose correspondence with contemporaries, whose views on others' writings, or whose influence on later writers are the subjects of Hayek's scholarship.

The writer who figures in all of these categories is John Stuart Mill. Hayek contributed an introduction to Mill's *Spirit of the Age* (E-9, 1942), edited Mill's correspondence with John Rae (A-52, 1943), edited Mill's notes on Senior's work (A-57, 1945), wrote an introduction to his *Earlier Letters* (A-107, 1963), and published the book on *John Stuart Mill and Harriet Taylor* (B-8, 1951).

Writers in the category "ideas only" include David Hume (A-108, 1963; B-11, B-12, B-13); Comte and Hegel (A-70, 1951) and the physicist Ernst Mach (A-119, 1967). Encyclopedia articles are devoted to Hermann Gossen, Henry Macleod, George W. Norman, Eugen v. Philippovich (*Encyclopaedia of the Social Sciences*), David Ricardo (*Chambers'*), Bernard Mandeville (*Handwörterbuch*) and Carl Menger (*International Encyclopedia of the Social Sciences*). The lives and works of some of these writers were also treated by Hayek in other publications: Gossen in a book edited by Hayek (E-1,

1927), Menger in a well-known article (A-25, 1934), and Mandeville in an address to the British Academy (A-116, 1966). Others whom Hayek treated biographically include Friedrich von Wieser in an introduction to his collected essays (E-2, 1929) and in an article (A-4, 1926); Richard Cantillon (E-3, 1931) and Henry Thornton (E-8, 1939) in introductions to works of theirs; Richard v. Strigl, Wesley Clair Mitchell, and Bruno Leoni in obituary articles (A-54, 1944, A-64, 1948, and A-122, 1968).

The Austrian School was treated by Hayek in two articles for encyclopedias (A-103, 1962, and A-124, 1968), but a much more detailed treatment was given to the French Ecole Politechnique, especially Saint-Simon and Auguste Comte, in an article in three parts under the title "The Counter-Revolution of Science" (A-42, 1941). This study (of over 100 printed pages) succeeded in showing a scientific movement of the past in an altogether new light; it was reprinted as a book (B-9) and appeared also in an abridged translation in French (1953) and in a complete translation in German (1959).

## Intellectual History Embodied in Every Treatise

It would not be possible in the present review to enumerate the instances in which Hayek presented the histories of particular ideas in his various articles and books in legal, political and social philosophy as well as in economics. Perhaps, however, I should mention a few of the great thinkers or schools of thought whose views Hayek analyzed in the context of his learned discourses: Descartes, the French Enlightenment, especially d'Alembert and Condorcet, Rousseau, the Physiocrats, Adam Smith, Bentham and the English Utilitarians, Lord Acton, de Tocqueville, Burke, and Locke.

## An Essay in Psychology

The record of Hayek's work would be incomplete if it failed to include mention of a book of his in the field of psychology. I have no competence in this field and cannot arrogate to myself the right to pass judgment on this work.

It appeared in 1952 under the title *The Sensory Order* (B-10). The book was reviewed with respect and partial acclaim by eminent psychologists, e.g., Edwin G. Boring *(The Scientific Monthly*, March 1953, pp. 182-183), but, as far as I know, it has not had much influence on professional psychologists.

## Philosophy of Science

Hayek's concern with philosophy of science in general and methodological problems of the social sciences in particular derived from his dissatisfaction with the assertions and prescriptions of social scientists regarding the "right" methods of inquiry. There were, on the one hand, those who thought that the methods of the natural sciences, especially physics, should be imitated in the social sciences; on the other hand, there were those who denied economics the status of a "science" and wanted its investigations to employ the working methods of the historians. As Hayek attempted to sort out and analyze the methodological problems of the social sciences, he found it necessary to become himself a philosopher of science.

Much of Hayek's thinking in this area is contained in his books and articles on substantive problems or on intellectual history. For example, while I chose to include his long essay on "The Counter-Revolution of Science" (A-42, 1941), among his work on history of ideas, one might with almost equal justification include it under the heading of philosophy of science. An even earlier publication, "Economics and Knowledge" (A-34, 1937), which I mentioned in the section on Socialism, Planning, and Competitive Capitalism, contains highly significant methodological suggestions. But instead of culling Hayek's ideas on the philosophy of science from a variety of his writings, I shall concentrate here on the essays and articles that are primarily or exclusively devoted to it.

### Critique of Scientism

His first major essay in this category is on "Scientism and the Study of Society" (A-46, 1942-1944), a critique of the "slavish imitation of the method and language of Science" (i.e., natural sciences) in the study of society. To guard against misunderstanding, Hayek assures us that his criticisms are not aimed "against the methods of Science in their proper sphere" or "to throw the slightest doubt on their value." He adds that "the scientistic as distinguished from the scientific view is . . . a very prejudiced approach which, before it has considered its subject, claims to know what is the most appropriate way of investigating it" (p. 269). The pejorative term "scientism" had been used in French writings, as Hayek tells us with supporting documentation.

In the preface to his book of collected essays, *Studies in Philosophy, Politics, and Economics* (B-13, 1967), Hayek calls attention (p. viii) to

> a slight change in the tone of my discussion of the attitude which I then called "scientism." The reason for this is that Sir Karl Popper has taught me that natural scientists did not really do what most of them not only told us that they did but also urged the representatives of other disciplines to imitate. The difference between the two groups of disciplines has thereby been greatly narrowed and I keep up the argument only because so many social scientists are still trying to imitate what they wrongly believe to be the methods of the natural sciences.

The essay on "Scientism" gives a clear account of the reasons why some of the rules of procedure claimed to be those of Science are inapplicable, or applicable only after appropriate modification, to the study of social phenomena. There is first the recognition that the "facts" of the social sciences are "opinions—not opinions of the student of social phenomena, of course, but opinions of those whose actions produce his object." Moreover, we cannot "observe" these opinions—our data—directly "in the minds of the people but [only] recognize [them] from what they do and say merely because we have ourselves a mind similar to theirs" (A-46, p. 279). Examples: sentences, crime, punishment, medicine, cosmetic, commodity, economic good, money, exchange, games, rent, scarcity, utility, price, cost, profit, etc., are all "opinions" of people. Hayek stresses the contrast "between ideas which by being held by the people become the causes of a social phenomenon and the ideas which people form about that phenomenon" (p. 285).

A thought which Hayek elaborates also in other contexts is formulated here with great clarity (p. 288):

> If social phenomena showed no order except insofar as they were consciously designed, there would indeed be no room for theoreti-

cal sciences of society and there would be, as is often argued, only problems of psychology. It is only in so far as some sort of order arises as a result of individual action but without being designed by any individual that a problem is raised which demands a theoretical explanation.

The difficulty with such "order" or "regularity" is that it "cannot be stated in physical terms, that if we define the elements in physical terms no such order is visible, and that the units which show an orderly arrangement do not (or at least need not) have any physical properties in common. . . ."

Hayek makes a "distinction between an explanation merely of the principle on which a phenomenon is produced and an explanation which enables us to predict the precise results" (p. 290) and, as an illustration of the former, he refers to "a set of equations which shows merely the form of a system of relationships but does not give the values of the constants contained in it" (p. 291).

I am tempted to quote many of Hayek's statements on behaviorism and physicalism; on attempts to explain mental processes by physical ones; on social wholes, which are not observable but are constructions of our minds to schematize supposed structures of relationships among selected actions and events; on the nature of statistical studies of social phenomena; on the claims and failures of historicism; on the complementarity between theoretical and historical work; on alleged laws of historical change and development; and on many other methodological problems with which he deals in this essay. I must not yield to this temptation, or this review will be far too long.

Hayek's distinction between scientific and scientistic attitudes has been widely accepted. More than 25 years after the publication of this lengthy essay, he was asked to write an article on "scientism" for a German encyclopedia of sociology (A-126, 1969).

*Explanation, Prediction, and Specialization*

Between 1943 and 1969 Hayek published another eleven essays in philosophy of science, seven in English, three in German, and one in French. Six of these essays were collected in his book *Studies in Philosophy, Politics and Economics*

(B-13, 1967). They were on "Degrees of Explanation" (A-76, 1955), "The Dilemma of Specialization" (A-80, 1956), "Rules, Perception and Intelligibility" (A-102, 1962), "The Theory of Complex Phenomena" (A-109, 1964), "Kinds of Rationalism" (A-112, 1965), and "The Results of Human Action but Not of Human Design" (A-118, 1967).

In the first of these essays, Hayek distinguishes positive and negative predictions, with those of disjunctive alternatives between the two. He stresses the difficulty, in as complex situations as economics presents, "that we are unable to ascertain by observation the presence and specific arrangement of the multiplicity of factors which form the starting point of our deductive reasoning" (A-76, p. 216). Falsification of a theory is not thereby excluded:

> Our tentative explanation will thus tell us what *kinds* of events to expect and which not, and it can be proved false if the phenomena observed show characteristics which the postulated mechanism could not produce.

But, in contrast with

> the supposedly normal procedure of physics . . . we do here not *invent* new hypotheses or constructs but merely *select* them from what we know already about some of the elements of the phenomena; in consequence we do not ask whether the hypotheses we used are true or whether the constructs are appropriate, but whether the factors we have singled out are in fact present in the particular phenomena we want to explain, and whether they are relevant and sufficient to explain what we observe.

In lieu of offering more quotations, attention may be called to Hayek's discussion of various issues of interest to particular groups of readers: illustrations of "explanations of the principle" (in contrast with explanations of particular observations), especially with reference to the theory of evolution by natural selection (pp. 218-220); the use of models for the explanation of "ranges of phenomena" and the problems of refuting their relevance, especially if they yield mostly "negative predictions" (pp. 220-224); the importance of "orientation" where prediction is not possible, and of "cultivation" where control is beyond our capacity (p. 225).

A few valuable insights may be presented here from Hayek's "Dilemma of Specialization" (A-80, 1956). He discusses the differences in the significance to different fields of inquiry of the "concrete and particular as against the general and theoretical" (p. 463), and the consequences of "exclusive concentration on a specialty":

> The physicist who is only a physicist can still be a first-class physicist and a most valuable member of society. But nobody can be a great economist who is only an economist—and I am even tempted to add that the economist who is only an economist is likely to become a nuisance if not a positive danger.

And (p. 464)

> The degree of abstraction which the theoretical disciplines in our field requires makes them at least as theoretical, if not more so, than any in the natural sciences. This, however, is precisely the source of our difficulty. Not only is the individual concrete instance much more important to us than it is in the natural sciences, but the way from the theoretical construction to the explanation of the particular is also much longer.

Furthermore (p. 465),

> most successful research work will require a very particular combination of diverse kinds of knowledge and accomplishments, and it may take half a lifetime until we are better than amateurs in three-quarters of the knowledge demanded by the task we have set ourselves.

Unfortunately (p. 465), "not every legitimate research specialty is equally suitable as a scientific education." Hayek concludes (pp. 469-70) that in economics

> we do not know as sharp a division between the theoretician and the practitioner as there exists between the physicist and the engineer or between the physiologist and the doctor. This is not an accident or merely an earlier stage of development but a necessary consequence of the nature of our subject. It is due to the fact that the task of recognizing the presence in the real world of the conditions corresponding to the various assumptions of our theoretical schemes is often more difficult than the theory itself, an art which only those will acquire to whom the theoretical schemes have become second nature. . . . We can, therefore, only rarely delegate the application of our knowledge but must be our own practitioners, doctors as well as physiologists.

### Action and Perception

Of the essay on "Rules, Perception and Intelligibility" (A-102, 1962) I shall only draw attention to Hayek's important observations on "rule-guided action" and "rule-guided perception," neither of which presupposes that we can state or describe the rules that guide our actions and perceptions. I

should like to make Hayek's statements of these issues required reading for any one who undertakes to talk or write
about the methodology of the social sciences.

The theme of the existence of subconscious rules that guide
perception is further elaborated in a brief essay on "The
Primacy of the Abstract" (A-128, 1969). Here Hayek defends
the proposition that perception of the concrete presupposes
an organizing capacity of the mind; this is what he means by
"primacy of the abstract." Hayek refers to the well-estab-
lished fact that "most animals recognize . . . abstract features
long before they can identify particulars." He goes back to
the writings of many important authors, from Adam Ferguson
(1767) through Immanuel Kant and Charles S. Peirce to quite
recent psychologists, zoologists, and ethologists, to show that
this recognition, although it contradicts a common textbook-
lesson, has been of rather old vintage, forgotten or disregarded
by the believers in the primacy of the concrete.

## Final Assessment

Where do Hayek's greatest achievements lie? Any judgment
of this sort will reflect the appraiser's personal interests and
tastes, especially in the case of a scholar like Hayek whose
work has been on so large a variety of subjects in several
fields. We can make our assessment somewhat easier if we
confine ourselves to Hayek's contributions to economic science.

There is still the choice among at least three or four
possibilities: the theory of economic fluctuations; the pure
theory of capital; the theory of economic planning under
socialism and competitive capitalism; and the methodology of
economics. If I had to single out the area in which Hayek's
contributions were the most fundamental and pathbreaking, I
would cast my vote for the theory of capital. As I said
before, when I reviewed Hayek's book on *The Pure Theory
of Capital*, it is "my sincere conviction that this work contains some of the most penetrating thoughts on the subject
that have ever been published."

If two achievements may be named, I would add Hayek's
contributions to the theory of economic planning. Most of

what has been written on systems analysis, computerized data processing, simulation of market processes, and other techniques of decision-making without the aid of competitive markets, appears shallow and superficial in the light of Hayek's analysis of the "division of knowledge," its dispersion among masses of people. Information in the minds of millions of people is not available to any central body or any group of decision-makers who have to determine prices, employment, production, and investment but do not have the signals provided by a competitive market mechanism. Most plans for economic reform in the socialist countries seem to be coming closer to the realization that increasing decentralization of decision-making is needed to solve the problems of rational economic planning.

## BIBLIOGRAPHY

*Books*

B-1.   *Geldtheorie und Konjunkturtheorie* (Vienna and Leipzig, 1928), xii, 147 pp. English edition, 1933. Japanese edition, 1935. Spanish edition, 1936. 2nd Austrian edition, 1976.

B-2.   *Prices and Production* (London, 1931), xv, 112 pp., 2nd revised and enlarged edition (London 1935), xiv, 162 pp. Austrian edition, 1931. Japanese edition, 1934. French edition, 1975.

B-3.   *Monetary Nationalism and International Stability* (Geneva, 1937), xiv, 94 pp. American edition, 1974.

B-4.   *Profits, Interest and Investment* (London, 1939), viii, 266 pp.

B-5.   *The Pure Theory of Capital* (London, 1941), xxxi, 454 pp. Spanish edition, 1946. Japanese edition, 1952.

B-6.   *The Road to Serfdom* (London and Chicago, 1944), 250 pp. Austrian edition, 1944. Swedish edition, 1944. French edition, 1945. German editions, 1945, 1952, 1971. Danish edition, 1946. Portuguese edition, 1946. Spanish edition, 1946. Netherlandish edition, 1948. Norwegian edition, 1949. Japanese edition, 1954. Chinese edition, 1956.

B-7.   *Individualism and Economic Order* (London and Chicago, 1948), vii, 271 pp. German edition, 1952.

B-8.   *John Stuart Mill and Harriet Taylor* (London and Chicago, 1951), 320 pp.

B-9.   *The Counter-Revolution of Science* (Glencoe, Ill., 1952), 255 pp. German edition, 1959. French excerpts, 1953.

B-10.  *The Sensory Order* (London and Chicago, 1952), xxii, 209 pp.

B-11.  *The Political Ideal of the Rule of Law* (Cairo, 1955), 60 pp. Partially reproduced, under the title *The Rule of Law*, by the Institute for Humane Studies, 1975.

B-12. *The Constitution of Liberty* (London and Chicago, 1960), x, 569 pp.

B-13. *Studies in Philosophy, Politics and Economics* (London and Chicago, 1967), x, 356 pp.

B-14. *Freiburger Studien: Gesammelte Aufsätze* (Tübingen, 1969), 284 pp.

B-15. *Law, Legislation and Liberty*, Vol. 1, *Rules and Order* (Chicago, 1973), xi, 184 pp.

*Pamphlets*

P-1. *Das Mieterschutzproblem: Nationalökonomische Betrachtungen* (Vienna, 1928).

P-2. *Freedom and the Economic System* (Chicago, 1939), iv, 38 pp.

P-3. *The Case of the Tyrol* (London, 1944).

P-4. *Reports on the Changes in the Cost of Living in Gibraltar 1939-1944 and on Wages and Salaries* (Gibraltar, no date [1945]).

P-5. *Individualism: True and False* (Dublin, 1946), 38 pp.

P-6. *Wirtschaft, Wissenschaft und Politik* (Freiburg, 1963), 24 pp.

P-7. *Was der Goldwährung geschehen ist. Ein Bericht aus dem Jahre 1932 mit zwei Ergänzungen.* Walter Eucken Institut: Vorträge und Aufsätze, 12 (Tübingen, 1965), 33 pp.

P-8. *The Confusion of Language in Political Thought, With Some Suggestions for Remedying It.* Institute of Economic Affairs, Occasional Paper 20 (London, 1968), 36 pp.

P-9. *Der Wettbewerb als Entdeckungsverfahren* (Kiel, 1968), 20 pp.

P-10. *Economic Freedom and Representative Government.* Fourth Wincott memorial lecture delivered at the Royal Society of Arts, Oct. 31, 1973 (London, 1973), 22 pp.

*Books Edited or Introduced*

E-1. Hermann Heinrich Gossen, *Entwicklung der Gesetze des menschlichen Verkehrs*, 3rd ed. (Berlin, 1927), xxiii, 278 pp. Introduction by F. A. H.

E-2. Friedrich Freiherr von Wieser, *Gesammelte Abhandlungen* (Tübingen, 1929), xxxiv, 404 pp. Edited with an introduction by F. A. H.

E-3. Richard Cantillon, *Abhandlung über die Natur des Handels im Allgemeinen*, translated by Hella von Hayek (Jena, 1931), xix, 207 pp. Introduction and annotations by F. A. H.

E-4. *Beiträge zur Geldtheorie* by Marco Fanno, Marius W. Holtrop, Johan G. Koopmans, Gunnar Myrdal, Knut Wicksell (Vienna, 1931), ix, 511 pp. Edited and Preface by F. A. H.

E-5. *Collectivist Economic Planning* (London, 1935), v, 293 pp. Edited with introductory and concluding chapters by F. A. H. French edition, 1939. Italian edition, 1946.

E-6. Boris Brutzkus, *Economic Planning in Soviet Russia* (London, 1935), xvii, 234 pp. Edited with a Preface by F. A. H.

E-7. *The Collected Works of Carl Menger*, 4 vols. (London, 1934-36). Introduction by F. A. H. German edition: Carl Menger, *Gesammelte Werke* (Tübingen, 1968 *et seq.*) Edited and introduced by F. A. H.

E-8.    Henry Thornton, *An Enquiry into the Nature and Effects of the Paper Credit of Great Britain* (1802). (London, 1939), 368 pp. Edited with an Introduction by F. A. H.

E-9.    *John Stuart Mill, The Spirit of the Age* (Chicago, 1942), xxxiii, 93 pp. Introduction by F. A. H.

E-10.   *Capitalism and the Historians* (London and Chicago, 1954), 188 pp. Edited with an Introduction by F. A. H.

*Articles in Learned Journals or Collections of Essays*

A-1.    "Das Stabilisierungsproblem in Goldwährungsländern," *Zeitschrift für Volkswirtschaft und Sozialpolitik*, N.S. 4 (1924).

A-2.    "Die Währungspolitik der Vereinigten Staaten seit der Überwindung der Krise von 1920," *Zeitschrift für Volkswirtschaft und Sozialpolitik*, N.S. 5 (1925).

A-3.    "Bemerkungen zum Zurechnungsproblem," *Jahrbücher für Nationalökonomie und Statistik*, 124 (1926).

A-4.    "Friedrich Freiherr von Wieser," *Jahrbücher für Nationalökonomie und Statistik*, 125 (1926).

A-5.    "Zur Problemstellung der Zinstheorie," *Archiv für Sozialwissenschaften und Sozialpolitik*, 58 (1927).

A-6.    "Das intertemporale Gleichgewichtssystem der Preise und die Bewegungen des Geldwertes," *Weltwirtschaftliches Archiv*, 28 (1928).

A-7.    "Einige Bemerkungen über das Verhältnis der Geldtheorie zur Konjunkturtheorie," *Schriften des Vereins für Sozialpolitik*, 173/2 (1928); also discussion, *loc. cit.*, 175 (1928).

A-8.    "Theorie der Preistaxen" (in Hungarian; reprint in German), *Häzgasdasagi Enciclopedia* (Budapest, 1929).

A-9.    "Gibt es einen Widersinn des Sparens?" *Zeitschrift für Nationalökonomie*, 1 (1929)—English: "The Paradox of Saving," *Economica*, 11 (1931).

A-10.   "Reflections on the Pure Theory of Money of Mr. J. M. Keynes," *Economica*, Part I, 11 (1931); Part II, 12 (1932).

A-11.   "The Pure Theory of Money: A Rejoinder to Mr. Keynes," *Economica*, 11 (1931).

A-12.   "Money and Capital: A Reply to Mr. Sraffa," *Economic Journal*, 42 (1932).

A-13.   "Kapitalaufzehrung," *Weltwirtschaftliches Archiv*, 36 (1932/II).

A-14.   "A Note on the Development of the Doctrine of 'Forced Saving'," *Quarterly Journal of Economics*, 47 (1932).

A-15.   "Gossen, Hermann Heinrich," *Encyclopaedia of the Social Sciences*, vol. VI (New York, 1932).

A-16.   "Macleod, Henry D.," *Encyclopaedia of the Social Sciences*, vol. X (New York, 1935).

A-17.   "Norman, George W.," *Encyclopaedia of the Social Sciences*, vol. XI (New York, 1933).

A-18.   "Philippovich, Eugen von," *Encyclopaedia of the Social Sciences*, vol. XII (New York, 1934).

A-19.   "Saving," *Encyclopaedia of the Social Sciences*, vol. XIII (New York, 1934).

A-20.   "The Trend of Economic Thinking," *Economica*, 13 (1933).

A-21.   Contribution to: *Der Stand und die nächste Zukunft der Konjunkturforschung. Festschrift für Arthur Spiethoff* (Munich, 1933).

A-22.   "Über 'Neutrales Geld'," *Zeitschrift für Nationalökonomie*, 4 (1933).

A-23.   "Capital and Industrial Fluctuations," *Econometrica*, 2 (1934).

A-24.   "On the Relationship between Investment and Output," *Economic Journal*, 44 (1934).

A-25.   "Carl Menger," *Economica*, N.S. 1 (1934).

A-26.   "Preiserwartungen, Monetäre Störungen und Fehlinvestitionen," *Nationalökonomisk Tidskrift*, 73 (1935).

A-27.   "The Maintenance of Capital," *Economica*, N.S. 2 (1935).

A-28.   "Spor miedzy szkola 'Currency' i szkola 'Banking'," *Ekonomista*, 55 (Warsaw, 1935).

A-29.   "Edwin Cannan" (obituary), *Zeitschrift für Nationalökonomie*, 6 (1935).

A-30.   "Technischer Fortschritt und Überkapazität," *Österreichische Zeitschrift für Bankwesen*, 1 (1936).

A-31.   "The Mythology of Capital," *Quarterly Journal of Economics*, 50 (1936). Reprinted in William Fellner and Bernard F. Haley, eds., *Readings in the Theory of Income Distribution* (Philadelphia, 1946).

A-32.   "Utility Analysis and Interest," *Economic Journal*, 46 (1936).

A-33.   "La situation monetaire internationale," *Bulletin Périodique de la Societé Belge d'Etudes et d'Expansion* (1936).

A-34.   "Economics and Knowledge," *Economica*, N.S. 4 (1937).

A-35.   "Einleitung zu einer Kapitaltheorie," *Zeitschrift für Nationalökonomie*, 8 (1937).

A-36.   "Das Goldproblem," *Österreichische Zeitschrift für Bankwesen*, 2 (1937).

A-37.   "Investment that Raises the Demand for Capital," *Review of Economic Statistics*, 19 (1937).

A-38.   "Economic Conditions of Inter-State Federation," *New Commonwealth Quarterly* (London), 5 (1939).

A-39.   "Pricing versus Rationing," *The Banker* (London), 51 (1939).

A-40.   "The Economy of Capital," *The Banker* (London), 52 (1939).

A-41.   "Socialist Calculation: The Competitive 'Solution'," *Economica*, N.S. 7 (1940).

A-42.   "The Counter-Revolution of Science," Parts I-III, *Economica*, N.S. 8 (1941).

A-43.   "Maintaining Capital Intact: A Reply to Professor Pigou," *Economica*, N.S. 8 (1941).

A-44.   "Planning, Science and Freedom," *Nature*, 148 (1941).

A-45.   "The Ricardo Effect," *Economica*, N.S. 9 (1942).

A-46.   "Scientism and the Study of Society," Part I: *Economica*, N.S. 9 (1942), Part II: *ibid.* 10 (1943), Part III: *ibid.* 11 (1944).

A-47.   "A Comment on an Article by Mr. Kaldor: 'Professor Hayek and the Concertina Effect'," *Economica*, N.S. 9 (1942).

A-48.   "A Commodity Reserve Currency," *Economic Journal*, 53 (1943).

A-49.   "The Facts of the Social Sciences," *Ethics*, 54 (1943).

A-50.   "The Geometrical Representation of Complementarity," *Review of Economic Studies*, 10 (1943).

A-51.   "Gospodarka planowa a idea planowania prawa," *Economista Polski* (London), (1943).

A-52.   Edited: "John Rae and John Stuart Mill: A Correspondence," *Economica*, N.S. 10 (1943).

A-53.   "The Economic Position of South Tyrol," in: *Justice for South Tyrol* (London, 1943).

A-54.   "Richard von Strigl" (obituary), *Economic Journal*, 54 (1944).

A-55.   "The Use of Knowledge in Society," *American Economic Review*, 35 (1945). Reprinted by the Institute for Humane Studies, 1971.

A-56.   "Time-Preference and Productivity: A Reconsideration," *Economica*, N.S. 12 (1945).

A-57.   Edited: " 'Notes on N. W. Senior's Political Economy' by John Stuart Mill," *Economica*, N.S. 12 (1945).

A-58.   "Nationalities and States in Central Europe," *Central European Trade Review* (London), 3 (1945).

A-59.   "Fuld Beskaeftigelse," *Nationalökonomisk Tidskrift*, 84 (1946).

A-60.   "The London School of Economics 1895-1945," *Economica*, N.S. 13 (1946).

A-61.   "Probleme und Schwierigkeiten der englischen Wirtschaft," *Schweizer Monatshefte*, 27 (1947).

A-62.   "Le plein emploi," *Economie Appliquée*, 1 (1948).

A-63.   "Der Mensch in der Planwirtschaft" in Simon Moser (ed.), *Weltbild und Menschenbild* (Innsbruck and Vienna, 1948).

A-64.   "Wesley Clair Mitchell 1874-1948" (obituary), *Journal of the Royal Statistical Society*, 111 (1948).

A-65.   "The Intellectuals and Socialism," *The University of Chicago Law Review*, 16 (1949). Reprinted by the Institute for Humane Studies, 1971.

A-66.   "Economics," *Chambers' Encyclopaedia*, vol. IV (Oxford, 1950).

A-67.   "Ricardo, David," *Chambers' Encyclopaedia*, vol. XI (Oxford, 1950).

A-68.   "Full Employment, Planning and Inflation," *Institute of Public Affairs Review* (Melbourne, Australia), 4 (1950).

A-69.   "Capitalism and the Proletariat," *Farmand* (Oslo), Feb. 17, 1951.

A-70.   "Comte and Hegel," *Measure* (Chicago), 2 (1951).

A-71.   "Comments on 'The Economics and Politics of the Modern Corporation'," *The University of Chicago Law School, Conference Series* no. 8, Dec. 7, 1951.

A-72.   "Die Überlieferung der Ideale der Wirtschaftsfreiheit," *Schweizer Monatshefte*, 32 (1952).

A-73.   "Die Ungerechtigkeit der Steuerprogression," *Schweizer Monatshefte*, 32 (1952).

A-74.   "Entstehung und Verfall des Rechtsstaatsideales," in *Wirtschaft ohne Wunder*, Albert Hunold, ed., Volkswirtschaftliche Studien für das Schweizerische Institut für Auslandforschung (Zürich, 1953).

A-75.   "Marktwirtschaft und Wirtschaftspolitik," *Ordo*, 6 (1954).

A-76.   "Degrees of Explanation," *The British Journal for the Philosophy of Science*, 6 (1955).

A-77.   "Towards a Theory of Economic Growth, Discussion of Simon Kuznets' Paper" in: *National Policy for Economic Welfare at Home and Abroad*. Columbia University Bicentennial Conference (New York, 1955).

A-78.   "Comments" in: Congress for Cultural Freedom (ed.), *Science and Freedom* (London, 1955). Proceedings of the Hamburg Conference of the Congress for Cultural Freedom. Also in German.

A-79.   "Reconsideration of Progressive Taxation," in Mary Sennholz (ed.), *On Freedom and Free Enterprise. Essays in Honour of Ludwig von Mises* (Princeton, 1956).

A-80.   "The Dilemma of Specialization" in Leonard D. White (ed.), *The State of the Social Sciences* (Chicago, 1956).

A-81.   "Über den 'Sinn' sozialer Institutionen," *Schweizer Monatshefte*, 36 (1956).

A-82.   "Was ist und was heisst 'sozial'?" in Albert Hunold (ed.), *Masse und Demokratie* (Zürich, 1957).

A-83.   "Grundtatsachen des Fortschritts," *Ordo*, 9 (1957).

A-84.   "Inflation Resulting from the Downward Inflexibility of Wages," in Committee for Economic Development (ed.), *Problems of United States Economic Development*, vol. I (New York, 1958).

A-85.   "La Libertad, La Economia Planificada y El Derecho," *Temas Contemporaneos*, 3 (1958).

A-86.   "The Creative Powers of a Free Civilization" in F. Morley (ed.), *Essays in Individuality* (Philadelphia, 1958).

A-87.   "Freedom, Reason, and Tradition," *Ethics*, 68 (1958).

A-88.   "Gleichheit, Wert und Verdienst," *Ordo*, 10 (1958).

A-89.   "Liberalismus (1) Politischer Liberalismus," *Handwörterbuch der Sozialwissenschaften*, vol. IV (Stuttgart-Tübingen-Göttingen, 1959).

A-90.   "Bernard Mandeville," *Handwörterbuch der Sozialwissenschaften*, vol. VII (Stuttgart-Tübingen-Göttingen, 1959).

A-91.   "Unions, Inflation and Profits" in Philip D. Bradley (ed.), *The Public Stake in Union Power* (Charlottesville, Va., 1959).

A-92.   "Freiheit und Unabhängigkeit," *Schweizer Monatshefte*, 39 (1959).

A-93.   "Verantwortlichkeit und Freiheit," in Albert Hunold (ed.), *Erziehung zur Freiheit* (Erlenbach-Zürich, 1959).

A-94.   "Marktwirtschaft und Strukturpolitik," *Die Aussprache*, 9 (1959).

A-95.   "An Röpke," in Wilhelm Röpke, *Gegen die Brandung* (Zürich, 1959).

A-96.   "The Free Market Economy: The Most Efficient Way of Solving Economic Problems," *Human Events*, 16 (1959).

A-97.   "The Social Environment" in B. H. Bagdikian (ed.), *Man's Contracting World in an Expanding Universe* (Providence, R.I., 1960).

A-98.   "The Corporation in a Democratic Society: In Whose Interest Ought It and Will It Be Run?" in M. Anshen and G. L. Bach (eds.), *Management and Corporations 1958* (New York, 1960).

A-99.   "The Non Sequitur of the 'Dependence Effect'," *The Southern Economic Journal*, 27 (1961).

A-100.  "Die Ursachen der ständigen Gefährdung der Freiheit," *Ordo*, 12 (1961).

A-101.  "The Moral Element in Free Enterprise" in National Association of Manufacturers (eds.), *The Spiritual and Moral Element in Free Enterprise* (New York, 1962).

A-102.  "Rules, Perception and Intelligibility," *Proceedings of the British Academy*, 48 (1962).

A-103.  "Wiener Schule," *Handwörterbuch der Sozialwissenschaften*, vol. XII (Stuttgart-Tübingen-Göttingen, 1962).

A-104.  "Alte Wahrheiten und neue Irrtümer" in *Das Sparwesen der Welt*, Proceedings of the 7th International Conference of Savings Banks (Amsterdam, 1963).

A-105.  "Arten der Ordnung," *Ordo*, 14 (1963). English version under the title "Kinds of Order in Society," *The New Individualist Review*, 3 (1964); reprinted by the Institute for Humane Studies, 1971.

A-106.  "Recht, Gesetz und Wirtschaftsfreiheit" in *Hundert Jahre Industrie und Handelskammer zu Dortmund 1863-1963* (Dortmund, 1963).

A-107.  Introduction to "The Earlier Letters of John Stuart Mill," *Collected Works of John Stuart Mill*, vol. XII (Toronto and London, 1963).

A-108.  "The Legal and Political Philosophy of David Hume," *Il Politico*, 28 (1963).

A-109.  "The Theory of Complex Phenomena" in Mario Bunge (ed.), *The Critical Approach to Science and Philosophy. In Honor of Karl R. Popper* (Glencoe, Ill., 1964).

A-110.  Parts of "Commerce, History of," *Encyclopaedia Britannica*, vol. VI (Chicago, 1964).

A-111.  "Die Anschauungen der Mehrheit und die zeitgenössische Demokratie," *Ordo*, 15/16 (1965).

A-112.  "Kinds of Rationalism," *The Economic Studies Quarterly* (Tokyo), 15 (1965).

A-113.  "Personal Recollections of Keynes and the 'Keynesian Revolution'," *The Oriental Economist*, 34 (1966).

A-114.  "The Misconception of Human Rights as Positive Claims," *Farmand*, Anniversary Issue (1966).

A-115.  "The Principles of a Liberal Social Order," *Il Politico*, 31 (1966). German translation in *Ordo*, 18 (1967).

A-116.  "Dr. Bernard Mandeville," *Proceedings of the British Academy*, 52 (1966).

A-117.  "L'Etalon d'Or—Son Evolution," *Revue d'Economie Politique*, 76 (1966).

A-118. "Résultats de l'action des hommes mais non de leurs desseins," in *Les Fondements Philosophiques des Systèmes Economiques*. Textes de Jacques Rueff et essais rédiges en son honneur (Paris, 1967).

A-119. Remarks on "Ernst Mach und das sozialwissenschaftliche Denken in Wien" in Ernst Mach Institut (ed.), *Symposium aus Anlass des 50. Todestages von Ernst Mach* (Freiburg i. B., 1967).

A-120. "Rechtsordnung und Handelnsordnung" in Erich Streissler (ed.), *Zur Einheit der Rechts- und Staatswissenschaften* (Karlsruhe, 1967).

A-121. "The Constitution of a Liberal State," *Il Politico*, 32 (1967). German translation in *Ordo*, 19 (1968).

A-122. "Bruno Leoni, the Scholar," *Il Politico*, 33 (1968).

A-123. "A Self-Generating Order for Society" in John Nef (ed.), *Towards World Community* (The Hague, 1968).

A-124. "Economic Thought, VI: Austrian School," *International Encyclopedia of the Social Sciences*, vol. IV (New York, 1968).

A-125. "Menger, Carl," *International Encyclopedia of the Social Sciences,* vol. X (New York, 1968).

A-126. "Scientismus" in W. Bernsdorf (ed.), *Wörterbuch der Soziologie*, 2nd ed. (Stuttgart, 1969).

A-127. "Three Elucidations of the 'Ricardo Effect'," *Journal of Political Economy*, 77 (1969).

A-128. "The Primacy of the Abstract" in Arthur Koestler and J. R. Smythies, (eds.), *Beyond Reductionism* (London, 1969).

A-129. "Il sistema concorrenziale come strumento di conoscenza" [The Competitive System as a Tool of Knowledge. (With English summary)], *L'industria* (Jan.-March 1970), 1, pp. 34-50.

A-130. "The Outlook for the 1970's: Open or Repressed Inflation?" in Sudha R. Shenoy (ed.), *A Tiger by the Tail: A 40-Years' Running Commentary on Keynesianism*. Hobart Paperback (London: Institute of Economic Affairs, 1972).

A-131. "Die Stellung von Mengers 'Grundsätzen' in der Geschichte der Volkswirtschaftslehre," *Zeitschrift für Nationalökonomie*, 32 (1), 1972. English version in J. R. Hicks and W. Weber, *Carl Menger and the Austrian School of Economics* (Oxford, 1973).

## Addenda

Between the completion of the bibliography and the preparation of this book of essays, the following publications of Hayek's writings have been noted:

*Pamphlets*

P-11.　*Full Employment at Any Price?* Institute of Economic Affairs, Occasional Paper 45 (London, 1975), 52 pp.

P-12.　*Choice in Currency: A Way to Stop Inflation*, Institute of Economic Affairs, Occasional Paper 48 (London, 1976), 29 pp.

*Articles in Learned Journals or Collections of Essays*

A-132.   "The Pretence of Knowledge," in *Les Prix Nobel en 1974*, Nobel
         Foundation, 1975; reprinted in Occasional Paper 45, Institute of Eco-
         nomic Affairs (London, 1975).

A-133.   "Die Erhaltung des liberalen Gedankengutes," in Friedrich A. Lutz (ed.),
         *Der Streit um die Gesellschaftsordnung* (Zürich, 1975).

A-134.   "Types of Mind," *Encounter*, 45 (September 1975).

A-135.   "A Discussion with Friedrich Hayek," American Enterprise Institute,
         Domestic Affairs Studies 39 (Washington, 1975).

A-136.   "The New Confusion about Planning," *The Morgan Guaranty Survey*
         (January 1976).

Arthur Shenfield

# Scientism and the Study of Society

We all have memories that mark certain turning points, or outstanding events, or peaks of experience, in our lives. From the many contributions to learning and enlightenment which we owe to Hayek, I have chosen *Scientism and the Study of Society* as the subject of this paper because for me it evokes just such a memory. In the 1930s I was aware of the illumination that Hayek spread about him but, bright though he shone, I thought of him only as an associate star to the brightest star among the economists of the time, namely, as I then believed, Lionel Robbins. For on first reading Robbins' *The Nature and Significance of Economic Science* I had felt "like some watcher of the skies when a new planet swims into his ken." Hayek, I then thought, was not quite as brilliant a planet as Robbins.

Had I read *The Pure Theory of Capital* when it appeared (1941), I might perhaps have changed my mind at that time, but I did not. I did not come upon it until a considerable time after the war, by which time my mind had already been changed for me. In 1942-44 *Scientism and the Study of Society* appeared in three parts in *Economica*. When I read them I became stout Cortez (or Balboa) on his peak in Darien. To this day I remember the tingling excitement which they evoked in me. Since then, the roll call of Hayek's works on the fundamental problems of society arouses in those who grasp their message a peak of admiration which is now familiar.

In 1942-44 we were all involved in momentous events. Our lives and liberties were in the balance. In such situations it is tempting to see the source of our peril in ideological error. Thus in the First World War L. T. Hobhouse wrote his famous *Metaphysical Theory of the State* to show that it was Hegel whom we were fighting. Though there was much truth in his argument, it was not quite fair either to Hegel or to the Kaiser's Germany. So too in 1942-44 one could not help seeing a connection between the barbarism menacing us in the Second World War and the scientism that Hayek dissected so brilliantly. But in so doing one was probably more correct than Hobhouse had been. Not that scientism was the barbarism's only source. Of course that was not the case. There were many strands in Nazism. Indeed, though historicism, which as we shall see is a leading element in scientism, was without doubt more deeply rooted in Germany than elsewhere, the other elements of scientism were just as popular an intellectual force in the western democracies as in Germany. In fact Hobhouse himself, considered to be a great liberal, was in many ways deeply infected with scientistic notions. And of course it is not to be forgotten that it was in France that scientism was first developed seriously and given a powerful impetus. Fortunately for the western democracies, in their milieu scientistic ideas, like other ideas making for totalitarianism, had to wrestle with ideas of a contrary character which still had a strong foothold, but which in Germany had mostly become submerged.

Before we proceed to examine the argument of *Scientism and the Study of Society*, we may take note of the fact that it was immediately followed in the wartime *Economica*, also in three parts, by Karl Popper's *The Poverty of Historicism*. Popper's articles have, I believe, achieved more fame than Hayek's.[1] If so, it is not easy to see why. The academic world appears rightly to have seen the articles on historicism as central to Popper's work, but wrongly to have regarded those on scientism as, at least in some measure, peripheral to Hayek's work.[2] Be that as it may, Popper's *Historicism* rein-

---

[1] When *The Counter-Revolution of Science* (Glencoe, Ill.: The Free Press, 1952), which included the article, "Scientism and the Study of Society," appeared in 1952 it was not even reviewed in the learned economic journals! Perhaps the editors looked at the title and decided that it had nothing to do with economics.

[2] Some weeks after I wrote this paper, I received a copy of Hayek's Nobel Memorial Lecture of December 11, 1974, "The Pretence of Knowledge," and found that its argument developed mainly from the exposure of the errors of scientism. It is clear that his exposure of these errors stands at the heart of Hayek's work.

forced Hayek's *Scientism*, even though Popper criticized
Hayek's exposition of certain points, notably his account of
the exact process by which the natural scientist reaches his
conclusions.[3] It is not an exaggeration to say that between
them Hayek and Popper have driven historicism out of the
intellectual field, except where Marxism still has some grip.
This is a most important achievement. For the influence of
historicism, especially in Germany, arose from its appeal to
scholars who had no sympathy for the main tenets of
Marxism. But the other elements of scientism have not been
exorcised. They are still with us, spread widely and in not
inconsiderable strength.

Scientism is the uncritical application of the methods, or of
the supposed methods, of the natural sciences to problems for
which they are not apt. In the present context it is their
application to problems of human society. Thus it is in its
very nature unscientific—an idolatry, not an understanding, of
science. As Hayek says, "The scientistic as distinguished from
the scientific view is not an unprejudiced but a very prejudiced approach which, before it has considered its subject,
claims to know what is the most appropriate way of investigating it."[4] And what is claimed to be the most appropriate
way turns out to be inappropriate.

Scientism would be an intellectual aberration if it were
always the application to the social sciences of the genuine
methods of the natural sciences. To a considerable extent,
however, it consists of the application of methods which arise
from a defective understanding of the ways of thinking in the
natural sciences. Thus, to this extent, it is doubly an aberration. As Hayek points out, ". . . the claims for the exclusive
virtues of the specific methods employed by the natural
sciences were mostly advanced by men whose right to speak
on behalf of the scientists was not above suspicion, and who

---

[3]Hayek accepted Popper's criticism on this point, for Popper persuaded him, as
he has taught and persuaded the rest of us, that the account of the methods of
science usually presented even by eminent and reputable natural scientists is
incorrect. [See the Preface to Hayek's *Studies in Philosophy, Politics and Economics* (London: Routledge & Kegan Paul, 1967), which is dedicated to Popper.]

[4]"Scientism and the Study of Society" in *The Counter-Revolution of Science*,
p. 16.

indeed in many cases had shown in the sciences themselves as much bigoted prejudice as in their attitude to other subjects."[5]

It is of course understandable that unschooled men should be so impressed by the immense success of the natural sciences as to leap to the conclusion that their methods hold the key to truth in all fields. But it is deplorable that men of scholarship should fall into the same trap, for the right path for the social sciences was opened up long ago by, among others, the early economists, especially Hume and Smith. Thus the scientistic attitude was a relapse from methods of inquiry whose fruitfulness had been well established. Of course the relapse was partially made possible by the affinity between scientism and some elements in the Cartesian heritage which held a stranglehold on the minds of many thinkers, especially in France. Hence it was in fact partly a revival of ways of thinking which had largely lain dormant in the social sciences during the period when the classical economists were blazing their pioneer trail.

Why is the application of the methods of the natural sciences, properly understood or not, to the social sciences an error? It is not because the most successful natural sciences study inanimate matter, for biology has also been splendidly successful. It is not because they mostly study non-human material, for the natural sciences of man, e.g., physiology, pathology, psychology, etc., hold an honorable place in the roll call of the sciences. It is not essentially because controlled experiment is available to the natural sciences but not to the social sciences, for there are cases where it is not available to the former but is available, even though the control may be loose, to the latter.

The error is perhaps best displayed by an examination of the leading features of the attitudes of scientism to the subject matter of social studies. The distinguishing marks of scientistic attitudes are, as described by Hayek, objectivism, collectivism, and historicism.

*Objectivism*[6] requires the student of society to stand out-

---

[5] *Op. cit.*, p. 14.
[6] It need hardly be said that this has nothing to do with the Objectivism of Ayn Rand.

side it, and to view it from that position, in the same way as the natural scientist stands outside the physical object, the plant or the animal that he studies. Hence to look inside a society to see what the individuals in it think about the very relations with each other which make it a society is, on this approach, no more legitimate or fruitful than would be an attempt to discover what atoms, molecules, genes or chromosomes thought about their relations with each other. Of course the objectivist may well look at the reactions of individuals, but only to external stimuli, as one may look at the reactions of atoms, molecules, genes, or chromosomes to external treatment or manipulation. In short the objectivist seeks to apply behaviorist principles to the activities of individuals, and if thereby he fails to find successful explanations of their behavior and of the nature of their society, he looks only to progress in the techniques or insights of behaviorism. This approach goes hand in hand often with a vague feeling, sometimes with a precise statement, that the social sciences must be based on the physical sciences. This calls in aid the progress of the physical sciences themselves to the point where in a sense they take over the social sciences, or lift the social sciences into their orbit. But this hope rests either on the belief that there can be no limits to the scope of the physical sciences, or on a simple neglect to consider where such limits may lie.

As was well understood by the pioneers of the study of society, and as Hayek has made more and more clear,[7] human society is the product of human action but not of human design. It arises from human action because individuals cooperate with each other without the stimulus or basis of a social contract or any idea of forming a whole society. The forms of cooperation are various and fluid, but out of them there arises a society which, in taking shape, develops institutions and rules which then become its distinguishing marks. The process may be masked by the emergence of a great law giver who may appear to be the founder of the society, or by some cataclysmic event from which a society may appear to

---

[7] In his *Constitution of Liberty* and his *Law, Legislation and Liberty*.

arise ready-shaped Phoenix-like; but it is inconceivable that such events were not antedated by forms or customs of cooperation whose influence was carried forward beyond those events.

If societies arise out of the cooperation of individuals and if, as is clearly the case, a society is a system of continuing cooperation, it follows that the study of society must deal with subjective phenomena. Why do men cooperate? What choices do they make in their cooperation? What ideas do they have about the scope of cooperation, about the resources available to them to satisfy their wants, about the reactions of each other to what they do, that induce them to make their choices? How do these choices interact to produce a social result? These are the questions which pose themselves for the social scientist. The objectivist cannot answer them, partly because he wishes them away, and partly because he denies himself the introspection which would enable him to see, from his knowledge of his own choices in action, why other men make choices and act upon them.

The way in which men cooperate with each other because of ideas about resources and other men's actions is most clearly demonstrated by the formation of markets. In a market men cooperate with each other because thereby they see opportunities for the easier, surer or greater service of their ends. But no individual needs to see the full extent of the market, or needs to be conscious of being an element of what appears objectively to be a market. The student of markets thus looks at something which arises from human choice in action and which cannot be understood without seeing how the various choices interact, though no single choice is directed at the formation of the whole market. The "organized" markets (stock exchanges, produce markets, etc.) are not an exception to this. All markets develop rules—that is why a market is a kind of society—and "organized" markets merely have more developed and more precise rules than others. The "members" of the "organized" markets may be conscious of the existence and operations of all the other "members," but they never know, or seek to know, all the participants in their markets, who range all the way from the original producers of the commodities to the ultimate consumers.

Since choice in action arises from ideas, the study of society is the study of phenomena formed by subjective ideas. But not all ideas. As Hayek puts it,

> While in the natural sciences the contrast between the object of our study and our explanation of it coincides with the distinction between ideas and objective facts, in the social sciences it is necessary to draw a distinction between those ideas which are *constitutive* of the phenomena we want to explain and the ideas which either we ourselves or the very people whose actions we have to explain may have formed *about* these phenomena and which are not the cause of, but theories about, the social structures.[8]

By its nature objectivism erects measurability as the test of what is to be studied. Though eminent natural scientists (e.g., Lord Kelvin) have been known to say that measurement is the whole of science, they have been mistaken even in their own fields. Yet measurement looms so large in the natural sciences, and is so conducive to their success, that he who takes them as his model is sure to give measurability the highest preference. But as a society is not a system of quantities but a system of relationships, its essentials cannot be measured. Hence the objectivist, forever making his measurements, is constantly to be found searching for what masks, not exposes, the nature of what he studies.

The success of the subjectivist approach was long ago most clearly demonstrated in the case of the theory of value in economics. In fact the case of value shows how obfuscating the objectivist approach can be. For though Smith and the other classical economists were penetrating subjectivists in their understanding of society, they failed to carry their insight through to the problem of value. Hence they adopted a labor theory of value, which was objectivist in character. Thus economics was held back in a vital particular for a century, until the subjective theory of value enabled it to make its great leap forward. How different the world might

---

[8] "Scientism and the Study of Society," in *The Counter-Revolution of Science*, p. 36.

have been if, say, Ricardo had forestalled Walras, Menger, and Jevons, and Marxism could not have been born!

The critics of the itch for measurement sometimes extend their criticism to the use of mathematics in economics. But the cases are not on all fours. Measurement for the sake of measurement is worthless, and measurement of misleading or meaningless quantities may be worse than worthless. But since economics deals with relations rather than with quantities, mathematics is intrinsically suitable for its exposition. No doubt it may be in any given case an unnecessary, or perhaps an inferior, medium of exposition. No doubt also it may be used to examine hypothetical problems which could never arise in the real world and which economists accustomed to the use of ordinary language would not waste time upon. Yet there is a clear difference between mathematics, even when an ill-chosen tool, and measurement which, when based on a misunderstanding of its subject matter, must produce error.

*Collectivism* (perhaps better called holism, if we may borrow from the philosophers) goes hand in hand with objectivism. It treats as wholes conventional constructs like "the economy" or "capitalism," or groups like nations or classes, as if they were each invested with a single mind and acted accordingly. This is partly the result of the adoption of loose or naive popular language. Thus "France" exports $x$ litres of wine, or the "United States" produces $y$ tons of coal, or "the steel industry" employs $z$ workers; when, of course, it is certain people in the geographical area called France who export wine, certain people in the United States who produce coal, and certain people, artificially assembled under the name of the "steel industry," who separately employ the men who make up the number $z$.

Partly collectivism is the result of the use of language for a system of relationships similar to that applied to living things. Thus one may say meaningfully "capitalism arose, flourished, and decayed," just as one may say the same of an animal or plant. The concepts are quite different, but the similarity of language induces a picture of capitalism as a whole with an objective life of its own like that of the subject of biological study. Hence, for example, the ludicrous categories of "high capitalism," "finance capitalism," "late capitalism," etc., of the German Historical School, in which the essence of capitalism was completely missed precisely because its supposed forms were looked at from the outside as wholes.

Partly collectivism arises from the essential belief of philosophical holism, namely that wholes are more than the sum of their parts, and that the parts are less real than the wholes, being largely abstract analytical distinctions.[9] Of course it is not to be denied that the whole of a society is more than what the sum of its individuals would be if they had no contact with each other. Such a sum would not be a society at all. A society is not a collection of hermits. It is formed because individuals set up relations with each other. It is then not more than the total of its interconnected individuals, their systems of connection being a vital element in it. Thus to treat the whole as a reality and the individuals as an unreality, or as a lesser reality, is a fundamental misconception. As Popper says, ". . . the holistic way of thinking (whether about 'society' or about 'nature') so far from representing a high level or late stage of the development of thought, is characteristic of a pre-scientific age."[10]

Like objectivism, collectivism leads to an exaggerated belief in the importance of measurement as a mark of scientific status. But by treating the objects of its study as wholes, it is led to subject to measurement almost anything except their essence, namely the systems of connection between individuals which become visible only when the concept of wholes is abandoned.

Now, however, we must face a problem which Hayek's *Scientism* did not deal with, namely the question of the legitimacy or virtue of macroeconomics. Is not the whole of macroeconomics infected with the collectivism that Hayek condemns? In concerning itself with the "economies" of political entities, does it not treat them illegitimately as

---

[9] See General Smuts' address to the British Association for the Advancement of Science, 1929. Here General Smuts showed himself to be the outstanding philosopher-statesman of his generation, but perhaps not as good a philosopher as a statesman.

[10] "The Poverty of Historicism," *Economica*, August 1944, p. 126.

wholes? Are not the GNP, the national income, the general price level, etc., typical holistic fictions?

To limit one's study to what happens within a political area is not necessarily holistic, though it runs the risk of being so. Subjective ideas and choices in action may properly be studied while limiting the field of view to a political area, though, since each national society is part of a greater society, some part of the essence of the object of study will thereby be excluded from view. Nor is the GNP necessarily holistic. It is possible to think of a quantity as a sum of the products of the people in a political group or area without treating the group as if it were a whole with a nature distinct from its individuals. Of course the GNP may be illegitimately used in a holistic manner; and, of course, it may be that in practice, even with the best statistical refinements, the computation of the GNP is bound to be of so crude a character that wise economists would shun its use. Thus it may be useless or misleading. But neither of these objections makes it inevitably holistic or a fiction.

But the general price level surely is a holistic fiction. It is not that it masks the course of relative prices, which are the prices that mostly matter, for the student may have his eye both on relative prices and on the general price level at the same time. Nor is it that, like that of the GNP, its computation is necessarily crude in that it depends upon arbitrary statistical selection. This only means that, like the GNP, it may be useless or misleading. It is a fiction because there is no such thing as a general price level, or, inversely, as a general value of money. Money is a human tool. No human has ever used, or could ever use, money to buy the general index. Nor do all the people in the area concerned together use money to buy the index. For though the aggregation of incomes of a group of individuals (to form a national income) can be a reality, the aggregation of the transactions in which money exchanges for goods cannot. Hence the general level of prices is a fiction, and a holistic fiction because it sets up an imaginary whole which is different from the individual transactions that are supposed to form it.

Yet who can deny that the concept of the general price

level, and the quantity theory of money which goes with it
and is also essentially holistic, have been as enlightening in
economics as they have been misleading?[11] Of course the
phenomena of inflation and deflation cannot be understood
without the concentration of attention upon relative prices,
which quantity of money theorists have sometimes been
known sadly to neglect. Yet would we have progressed as far
as we have done in understanding them, if the quantity
theory had never been propounded?

It seems to me that here one has to admit a qualification to
Hayek's condemnation of collectivist notions. Those that he
had in mind undoubtedly produce egregious error. But there
may be a few collectivist, or near-collectivist, concepts which,
when used by those who know the pitfalls of collectivism,
may be enlightening. Macroeconomics can have value, but
only in the hands of those who are first and foremost micro-
economists.

*Historicism*, the third feature of the scientistic approach,
makes two assertions. First, that there are no general laws of
social behavior which apply to men in all societies or historical epochs. Thus, for example, no theory of price can hold
good both in a feudal and in a capitalist society. To deduce it
from the phenomenon of human—not feudal human or
capitalist human, but simply human—choice in action, as
economists do, is therefore illegitimate. Each epoch or stage
in social development is *sui generis*. The springs of action in it
can only be understood by the study of its institutions and
social and economic structure. Second, the only general law is
a law of history. This is the law which explains how one
historical stage of society develops into the next stage.

It would be difficult to discover two assertions more hope-
lessly false. On the one hand the approach by way of the
study of human action and the subjective ideas which motivate

---

[11] Consider Irving Fisher's statement, "I became increasingly aware of the
imperative need of a stable yardstick of value. I had come into economics from
mathematical physics, in which fixed units of measure contribute the essential
starting point," in *Stabilised Money*, p. 375, quoted in *Man, Economy, and State*,
by Murray Rothbard, p. 741. A more revealing scientistic statement could not be
imagined.

it has produced, at least in economics, a body of doctrine and knowledge as well established as any in the natural sciences. On the other hand for three-quarters of a century the German Historical School, and for at least a generation the American Institutionalists, produced countless studies of institutions and structures which have left us no legacy of insight or understanding. Perhaps the best illustration of this is the way in which the great German inflation of 1922-23 found the "economists" trained in the Historical School all at sea, helpless to explain the most shattering economic phenomenon of their time; while in Vienna those who had been trained in the subjectivist school provided the correct explanation. Similarly the American Institutionalists had nothing of value to say about the Great Depression. It is not surprising, therefore, that even in Wisconsin the Institutionalist School has faded away; and that in Germany the influence of the Historical School is largely spent, except in Marxist circles.

As for the idea that there is a theory of history leading us to a law or laws of historical development, it is not unfair to describe it as patent superstition. In the first place it is purely holistic in its view of the forms of development, and is vitiated by the blindness of holism. In the second place, since it postulates that men do what they do because they are shaped by the institutional structures of their societies, it has always been a mystery how the historicist, Marx, for example, was able to stand outside his society and see the hand of history writing its fate. As Hayek points out, the older Historical School was free from this superstition. But by promoting the view that each historical phase was unique in every respect, they opened the way to a quest for some theory other than that of the pioneer social scientists, and thus to a belief in a law or laws of history.

After an examination of the objectivism, collectivism, and historicism of scientism, Hayek shows how it leads to a demand for the "conscious" control, or direction, or planning of society, and thus to the terrible scourge of totalitarianism. Thus the connection between scientism and the menace of Nazism at Hayek's time of writing was real enough. It remains a powerful element in the trend to totalitarianism 30 years later.

# Ronald Max Hartwell

# Capitalism and the Historians

It may well be that we as scholars tend to overestimate the influence we can exercise on contemporary affairs. But I doubt whether it is possible to overestimate the influence which ideas have in the long run. And there can be no question that it is our special duty to recognise the currents of thought which still operate in public opinion, to examine their significance, and, if necessary, to refute them.[1]

## Relevant Questions

Are historians hostile to capitalism? And are their views influential in determining attitudes and policies towards capitalism? One of the themes of the Mont Pelerin Society meeting at Beauvallon in France in September 1951 was the treatment of capitalism by the historians and its significance. Three of the papers, and two earlier papers by members of the society, with an introduction by Hayek, were published in 1954 in the volume, *Capitalism and the Historians*.[2] Hayek, as editor, and the contributors—T. S. Ashton, L. M. Hacker, B. de Jouvenel and W. H. Hutt—argued that the historians generally had been hostile and unfair to capitalism, and had created historical myths that not only were erroneous, but also were harmful to capitalism and a free society. While the main indictment was directed at the historians, de Jouvenel argued for a more general malaise. "A large part of the Western intelligentsia of today," he wrote, "forms and conveys a warped picture of our economic institutions." While the roots of such antipathy were historical, it was not created by the historians. "Unfavourable views of capitalism, whole systems of thought directed against it, were prevalent in large

---

[1] F. A. Hayek, *The Counter-Revolution of Science* (Glencoe, Ill.: The Free Press, 1952), p. 206.

[2] F. A. Hayek (ed.), *Capitalism and the Historians* (London: Routledge and Kegan Paul, 1954).

sectors of the intelligentsia before historians exposed the past wrongs of capitalism or indeed before they paid any attention at all to social history." In de Jouvenel's view, the intellectuals threatened modern society just as they had been "the major agents in the destruction of the ancient structure of Western society."[3] In the same way Schumpeter in *Capitalism, Socialism, and Democracy* had argued in 1942 that capitalism would fail, not because of any inherent economic weakness, but because of the hostility roused and sustained by the intellectuals.[4] While Ashton, de Jouvenel, and Hacker demonstrated the anti-capitalist bias of the intellectuals and the historians, Hayek also stressed the importance of this bias in the formation of general anti-capitalist sentiments and in the consequent formulation and implementation of socialist policies. Hayek noted "the extent to which our present political beliefs are coloured by historical beliefs," and reckoned that "in the indirect and circuitous process by which new political ideas reach the general public, the historian holds a key position."[5] Hayek traced a line of causation, from the historian to the general public and to the politicians, so that the historians' prejudices were translated finally into socialist legislation.

*Capitalism and the Historians* raised a number of important problems still with us, problems that can be specified in the form of questions. Why is it, when it is obvious to a liberal* that everybody should approve of capitalism, that so many people, and so many intelligent and responsible people, do not? Why is it, when it is obvious to a liberal that socialism (the progressive transfer of decision making from the private to the public sector) is both economically inefficient and

---

[3] B. de Jouvenel, "The Treatment of Capitalism by Continental Intellectuals," in *Capitalism and the Historians*, pp. 100, 103, 122.

[4] J. A. Schumpeter, *Capitalism, Socialism, and Democracy* (London: George Allen and Unwin, 1943) chs. XII, XIII.

[5] *Capitalism and the Historians*, pp. 7, 8.

*In this essay the word "liberal" as a noun and/or adjective is used in the classical sense of referring to the freedom of the individual from coercion by the state and other power groups. Hence it means opposition to government intervention, and, therefore, the opposite of the modern American meaning of the word as favoring or demanding government interventions.

politically unfree, that so many people see it as a desirable alternative to capitalism? What historical process has eroded liberalism and strengthened socialism, both in the realm of ideas and in the practice of government? What historical forces have led to the remarkable expansion of the public sector, beginning in the nineteenth and accelerating in the twentieth century? To what extent has the growth of intervention and of the public sector been the result of the implementation by governments of theories about socialism, and to what extent the result of other factors (for example, the extension of executive authority to bureaucracies)? How widely are the consequences of socialism—"the road to serfdom" rather than "the road to the millennium"—known and appreciated?

This paper attempts to answer some of these questions, and to assess Hayek's contribution to our understanding of the anti-capitalist mentality and its influence.

## Capitalism and the Historians

Hayek is an economic and political theorist rather than an historian. Nevertheless *Capitalism and the Historians* is an important and influential book and most of Hayek's writing since the publication of *The Road to Serfdom*[6] in 1944 has been at least partly concerned with history. *The Road to Serfdom* undoubtedly marked a turning point in Hayek's intellectual development, beyond which he became increasingly concerned, not so much with analysis of market and command economic systems, but with determining the conditions of freedom, with the definition of constitutions that minimize the role of coercion in human affairs and that reduce human obstacles to the exercise of individual choice. In *The Road to Serfdom* Hayek shows the consequences of replacing "the impersonal and anonymous mechanism of the market by collective and 'conscious' direction of all social forces to deliberately chosen goals."[7] "The road to socialism," he demonstrated, at the same time creating a phrase that has passed into common usage, is "the road to serfdom." But, he

[6] F. A. Hayek, *The Road to Serfdom* (London: Routledge, 1944).
[7] *Ibid.*, p. 15.

also affirms, there is nothing inevitable about this road to socialism. It is, unfortunately in the democracies, a road freely taken. As Hayek claims, "It is because nearly everybody wants it that we are moving in this direction."[8] And in wanting socialism Hayek points out the particular importance of an intellectual leadership dominated by socialist ideals. "The important point is that, if we take the people whose views influence developments, they are now in the democracies in some measure all socialists."[9]

Hayek attacks socialism and defends freedom, not so much by the use of history as by economic and political analysis. In particular, he analyzes the consequences of socialism. "The main question"—answered in *The Road to Serfdom*—"is where the movement will lead us."[10] "Is there a greater tragedy imaginable," he concludes, "than that, in our endeavour consciously to shape our future in accordance with high ideals, we should in fact unwittingly produce the very opposite of what we have been striving for?"[11] Hayek also restates the case for liberalism—"the abandoned road"[12]— formulating "a new statement of the liberal principles of justice and political economy."[13] "My aim," he writes in *The Constitution of Liberty*, "is to picture an ideal, to show how it can be achieved, and to explain what its realization would mean in practice."[14] In *Law, Legislation and Liberty*, however, he goes farther than restating "the traditional doctrine of liberal constitutionalism," and asks "what constitutional arrangements, in the legal sense, might be most conducive to the preservation of individual freedom."[15]

Hayek in these writings sees himself as a political philosopher rather than as an historian, and certainly not as a

[8] *Ibid.*, p. 3.

[9] *Ibid.*, p. 3.

[10] *Ibid.*, p. 3.

[11] *Ibid.*, p. 4.

[12] The title of chapter 1 of *The Road to Serfdom*.

[13] The subtitle of *Law, Legislation and Liberty*.

[14] F. A. Hayek, *The Constitution of Liberty* (London: Routledge and Kegan Paul, 1960), p. vii.

[15] F. A. Hayek, *Law, Legislation and Liberty*, Vol. I, *Rules and Order* (London: Routledge and Kegan Paul, 1973), pp. 2, 3.

practical politician. "The task of the political philosopher," he writes, "can only be to influence public opinion, not to organize people for action."[16] His aim, nevertheless, is to change informed "public opinion" and, indirectly, political action. He argues strongly for the influence of ideas in historically shaping political and economic opinions; and he regards the "intellectuals"—"the professional secondhand dealers in ideas"—as decisively important in the propagation of ideas. For example, he reckons that "in every country that has moved towards socialism the phase in development in which socialism becomes a determining influence on politics has been preceded for many years by a period during which socialist ideals governed the thinking of the more active intellectuals."[17] Hence the importance of "the intellectuals," who in the democracies "have probably never exercised so great an influence as they do today."[18] But, while recognizing the power of the intellectuals to shape public opinion, and while analyzing some of the forces that have disposed the intellectuals towards socialism, Hayek is more interested in demonstrating the unfree tendencies of socialism, and in devising constitutional and legal blueprints for a free society, than in diagnosing *why* liberal beliefs have declined, and *why* socialist beliefs have advanced until today they dominate public policy.

Hayek recognizes the problem of a "widespread emotional aversion to 'capitalism' "[19] in the democracies, but only *Capitalism and the Historians* among his writings is concerned primarily with the origins of the anti-capitalist mentality, and, in particular, with the influence of history on the formation of opinions harmful to a free society.[20] Insofar as Hayek is interested in understanding and combating the opposition to capitalism, however, he might well have written more on this theme. As it is, his essay "History and Politics" is an illumi-

---

[16] *The Constitution of Liberty*, p. 411.

[17] "The Intellectuals and Socialism," in F. A. Hayek, *Studies in Philosophy, Politics and Economics* (London: Routledge and Kegan Paul, 1967), p. 178.

[18] *Ibid.*

[19] *Capitalism and the Historians*, p. 10.

[20] Hayek wrote only the introduction to *Capitalism and the Historians*, but this introduction was a substantial essay which, when reprinted in *Studies in Philosophy, Politics and Economics*, was entitled, significantly, "History and Politics."

nating analysis of the role of history in attitude formation. Much history, he points out, is mythology, and an established mythology about the industrial revolution and its effects on the working classes has biased the attitudes of generations against the achievements of nineteenth century liberalism, and has disposed those generations to be critical of capitalism and to believe that socialism must be more humane, more efficient, and, paradoxically, more free. Certainly the prevalence of these views, whatever their origins, constitutes a formidable obstacle to the acceptance of a liberal philosophy, and to the re-establishment of a liberal society in the democracies. Understanding the anti-capitalist mentality—tracing its history, identifying its support, measuring its influence, analyzing its arguments against capitalism—is a necessary prelude to the removal of that obstacle.

## The Anti-Capitalist Mentality

Is it a negative attitude towards capitalism rather than a positive attitude towards socialism that has eroded liberalism?[21] Certainly the strength and ubiquity of the opposition to capitalism is seldom acknowledged by those who support economic liberalism. And it is easier to denounce socialism than to explain why so many people reject capitalism. This rejection is an uncomfortable fact with which the liberal seems unwilling, or unable, to come to terms. The liberal, moreover, acts as though revealing the illiberal tendencies of socialism will lead all rational people to accept capitalism. This is, essentially, the Hayek position. But the opposition to capitalism is not rational in the sense understood by Hayek. The opponents of capitalism are generally not moved by liberal arguments about freedom and choice, the existence of which they reject as illusory or irrelevant. The opponents of

---

[21] I use the terms capitalism and socialism as shorthand descriptions of two opposing systems of social organization: *capitalism* based on private property, market economy, and minimum government; *socialism* on public ownership, command economy, and comprehensive intervention. There are, of course, intermediate positions with attitudes that can be described as pro-capitalism or pro-socialism depending on the unwillingness or willingness to use government intervention to "solve" social and economic "problems," and as an instrument of social engineering.

capitalism depend on a mutually reinforcing battery of facts, theories, and values that cannot be disturbed by contrary evidence, and are not susceptible to rational argument. It is a prime mistake of the liberal, therefore, to imagine that he can win the debate about "capitalism versus socialism" by the normal academic game of proving or disproving according to rules and logic. This is the practical weakness of Hayek's liberalism.

"The attribution of rationality to human nature," Keynes pointed out in a famous memoir, ignores ". . . certain powerful and valuable springs of feeling."[22] In the case of the opposition to capitalism those feelings include moral indignation, aesthetic revulsion, envy, and hate, as well as rational rejection of capitalism because of its alleged inefficiency. On moral indignation, nothing better has been written than R. H. Tawney's *The Sickness of an Acquisitive Society*, in which he alleged that "industrialised communities neglect the very objects for which it is worthwhile to acquire riches in their feverish pre-occupation with the means by which riches can be acquired. That obsession . . . is a poison which inflames every wound and turns each trivial scratch into a malignant cancer."[23] Aesthetic revulsion has been documented, for example, by F. D. Klingender, who argued that the industrial revolution produced "cashbox aesthetics," a decline in tastes and a growth of vulgarity, and, of course, a dramatic and usually unfortunate change in the environment.[24] On envy and hate, the original scenario was written by Engels, who argued in 1844 that "It is now too late for a peaceful solution. The classes are divided more and more sharply, the

---

[22] J. M. Keynes, *Two Memoirs* (London: Rupert Hart-Davis, 1949), p. 101. Keynes was concerned, in particular, with the attitude of D. H. Lawrence to the Bloomsbury Set. He recognized his own tendency to attribute "an unreal rationality to other people's feelings and behaviour (and doubtless to my own too)," and the tendency of the set to ignore "both the reality and the value of vulgar passions" (pp. 100, 103). There was, he concluded, "no solid diagnosis of human nature" underlying their comments "on life and affairs" (p. 102). Hence Lawrence's "passionate distaste" (p. 103).

[23] R. H. Tawney, *The Sickness of an Acquisitive Society* (London: Fabian Society, 1920), p. 86.

[24] F. D. Klingender, *Art and the Industrial Revolution* (London: Noel Carrington, 1947), p. 120.

spirit of resistance penetrates the workers, the bitterness intensifies, the guerilla skirmishes become concentrated in more important battles, and soon a slight impulse will suffice to set the avalanche in motion."[25] This assumption of inevitable class conflict with its overtones of envy and hatred has been repeated by a long line of historians since Engels, and is still widely accepted today.

The anti-capitalist mentality is also sustained by "a quasi-apocalyptic fantasy" that had its origins in a medieval religious vision of the millennium, a vision transformed and secularized in the nineteenth century by Marx. Socialists are, fundamentally, revolutionaries; they want to transform society, and so their opposition to capitalism is endowed with transcendental significance. Like the revolutionary messianism of the Middle Ages, so well described by N. Cohn, many socialists want not only to produce "the Heavenly City," paradise now with "aims and promises" that are "boundless," but usually to do so dramatically, "with a cataclysm from which the world is to emerge totally transformed and redeemed." There is in much of the rhetoric of the socialists "the tense expectation of a final, decisive struggle in which a world of tyranny will be overthrown by a 'chosen people,' and through which the world will be renewed and brought to a consummation."[26] Marx added to an ancient religious and revolutionary fervor a model of history that was both scientific and progressive, in which the enemies of progress were clearly identified, and in which the forces of history made progress inevitable. Socialist zeal for revolution was endowed with a progressive role in a comprehensive theory of history in which the socialist could see himself, not just as improving the conditions of the working classes, and as abolishing tyranny and exploitation, but as a necessary and beneficial vehicle of history. Thus passion combined with science to increase the appeal of socialism, and to help ensure its popularity, survival and continuing influence.

---

[25] F. Engels, *The Condition of the Working Class in England* (Henderson-Chaloner translation, Oxford: Basil Blackwell, 1958), p. 335.

[26] N. Cohn, *The Pursuit of the Millennium* (London: Mercury Books, 1962), pp. 307-309.

But not all, perhaps not the majority, of critics of capitalism have been revolutionaries or historicists[27] and not all are messianic utopians. Most of the critics of capitalism, at least in Great Britain, are reformers who accept capitalism but believe that it can be modified by government intervention in socially desirable ways. These critics, in fact, do not absolutely reject the liberal economy, and positively uphold liberalism in politics (as they see it), but they are concerned with problems of capitalist economy, and especially with its alleged inefficiencies and obvious inequalities. Among inefficiencies they point to the problems of dealing with public goods and public bads, to the trade cycle (endemic fluctuations with painful social consequences), to monetary instability, to the failure to achieve "optimum" growth, and to the wastage of physical and human resources. But, more important, they argue that capitalism fails to deal with persistent and socially unacceptable poverty, because as a system capitalism produces inequalities of income and wealth that are unjust and socially divisive. These are "problems" that rouse indignation and passion, yet are treated too lightly by the liberals, or too rationally. Hayek is no exception. To argue that "even the poorest today owe their relative material well-being to the results of past inequality," and that redistribution of income "cannot be based on any scientific argument but must be recognized as a frankly political postulate"[28]—correct though both statements are—does not convince those who reject inequality with a moral absolute. The reformers, in contrast, see such "problems" as practical problems to be solved, not intellectual problems to be explained. Fabianism (a theory of political reform without revolution, a policy of democratically achieved socialism) and the welfare state (the implementation of meliorist policies) have been the substantial achievements of the reformers. It is difficult to attack the welfare state—"that hodge-podge of ill-assembled and often

---

[27] The claim "to recognise necessary laws of historical development and to be able to derive from such insight knowledge of what institutions [are] appropriate to the existing situation." *The Constitution of Liberty*, p. 236.

[28] *The Constitution of Liberty*, pp. 44, 311.

inconsistent ideals"[29]—against those who accept it uncritically as morally justifiable. The reformers, nevertheless, are irrational in their rejection of what *is* in favor of what *might be* without adequate comparison of these alternatives. The reformers dislike capitalism, which they identify with existing economic and social conditions, and with conditions back to the beginnings of the industrial revolution (the period of modern capitalism), and they like socialism, which they see as a desirable alternative to capitalism. But whereas capitalism is seen realistically with all its faults, socialism is only vaguely specified; socialism exists rather as an ideal, not as a system that has been tried and proved workable, not as a system whose virtues and vices have been compared realistically with capitalism.[30] To compare the real faults of a system that is known with the alleged virtues of something not yet known, however, is to tilt the balance of approval decisively against the known.[31] To use such a comparison as the basis for policy is surely irrational and certainly irresponsible; at least it displays uncalculating optimism. With its promises of improvement, however, reform even with unspecified consequences, has powerful and widespread appeal; better the "heaven" that is not known than the "hell" that is.

## Social Inquiry and Intervention

Is it true, as Hayek claims, that we have socialism because "nearly everybody" wants socialism? Or is it rather, as is shown above, that we have socialism because "nearly everybody" rejects capitalism? Or have we got socialism by accident, a windfall consequence of democratic government? One thing is certain; the democracies and liberal economies have moved continuously towards socialism in the twentieth cen-

---

[29] F. A. Hayek, "*The Road to Serfdom* after Twelve Years," in *Studies in Philosophy, Politics and Economics*, p. 221.

[30] The existence of communist economies does not provide the empirical experience for democratic socialism. Most democratic socialists would reject such economies if only for their lack of political freedom. Indeed criticism of communism is almost as prevalent as criticism of capitalism by democratic socialists.

[31] As A. C. Pigou wrote in *Socialism versus Capitalism* (London: Macmillan, 1937), p. 135: "For we are setting a nude figure, with all its blemishes patent to the eye, against a figure that is veiled."

tury, towards increasing government intervention in economic affairs, and towards the enlargement of the public sector. The liberal economy seems to be in inexorable decline.[32] This decline, moreover, has occurred in the context of democratically elected governments which were responsible either for intervention or for allowing the autonomous growth of bureaucratic intervention. To this extent Hayek is correct. But why did governments become increasingly interventionist? Not only because the majority of the electorate wanted it. Governments intervened also for doctrinal reasons (belief in socialism, although there has not been in the democracies much overall planning), partly as a response to revealed social problems, and partly because they could afford it. To an important extent, however, government grew in the nineteenth century to remedy social and economic problems which were exposed by public inquiry.[33] This process can be seen most clearly in Britain,[34] where it is easy to relate the growth of government to the social inquisitions initiated by parliament. Public inquiry was usually a symptom of conflict, and its function was to collect information and to suggest remedy. Public inquiries—parliamentary select committees and royal commissions of inquiry—were conflict- and problem-oriented (concerned with the ills of society, not its goods) and were biased in organization (dominated so often by interested parties), yet were the main source of information available to parliament about social and economic problems. And public inquiry was made

---

[32]Measured by a number of criteria—public expenditure as a percentage of national income, public employment as a percentage of total employment, the proportion of national income generated in the public sector, the number and size of nationalized industries and services—there has been a decline of private enterprise and a corresponding increase in public control. See, for example, G. W. Nutter, "The Trend: Where Are We Headed?" unpublished paper presented to the Southern Economic Association, 1974.

[33]See R. M. Hartwell, "Social Inquiry and the Growth of Government in Nineteenth Century Britain," paper presented to a meeting of The International Society for the History of Behavioral and Social Sciences, at Carleton University, Ottawa, June 1975.

[34]The same process can be seen elsewhere, for example in Europe. See E. N. and P. R. Anderson, *Political Institutions and Social Change in Continental Europe in the Nineteenth Century* (Berkeley: University of California Press, 1967), Ch. 5, "Bureaucracy." This book details the growth of bureaucracy but I do not in general agree with its interpretation of the results of that growth.

in the expectation of a public solution, government intervention by legislation and the establishment of a bureaucracy of supervision or control.

The most important discontinuity in British government, however, was not a willingness to inquire, or even to legislate, but to extend executive authority to the civil service. As MacDonagh has written: "Most historians take it for granted that the function and structure of executive government changed profoundly in the course of the nineteenth century. They would probably agree, moreover, that this change was revolutionary in a sense in which the changes of the seventeenth and eighteenth centuries, or even in the first half of the twentieth century were not; and also that it was revolutionary both in kind and in 'quantity.' "[35] What was unique was the willingness to extend executive authority, and to be able to afford and administer an expanding bureaucracy. Expansion of the bureaucracy depended not only on the compliance of parliament, and on the development of administrative and technical skills that permitted the extension of the old, or the introduction of new, areas of control, but also on finance. Heckscher once pointed out that mercantilist governments would have found it impossible to administer their laws, such were the size and expertise of their bureaucracies in comparison with the range and complexity of the laws. Laws in these circumstances were like moral precepts, binding but not systematically enforced, carrying penalties for noncompliance but not administered by an ever-watchful bureaucracy. A characteristic feature of nineteenth-century administration was its increasing professionalization, whether to organize a privately sponsored anti-Corn Law campaign, or to administer a public policy like that formulated in the Factory Acts. In the case of public administration professionalization was explicitly embodied in important reforms of the Civil Service which accompanied their expansion. But expertise was not costless. We know that there are no free lunches. Neither are there free bureaucracies; nor were there in the

---

[35] O. MacDonagh, "The Nineteenth-Century Revolution in Government: A Reappraisal," *Historical Journal*, I (1958), pp. 52-53.

nineteenth century. And although belief in *laissez-faire*, and reluctance by all chancellors of the exchequer to increase public expenditure, restrained government expansion, it would not halt it. After 1900, in the intellectual atmosphere of declining faith in market economy and *laissez-faire*, and with the relaxation of attitudes towards public expenditure, there was no such restraint. And so the twentieth century has been the century of "galloping government," of remarkable government growth unrestrained by ideals or income. The turning point, however, was the industrial revolution, which created or magnified social and economic problems, at the same time creating massive wealth. This increasing wealth of Britain broadened and deepened the tax base of government and, with economic growth and increasing population, government revenues grew almost involuntarily. In these circumstances the growth of bureaucracy was achieved initially, albeit grudgingly, without large increases in taxation.

And bureaucracies once created grew almost autonomously, primarily through a feedback mechanism whereby civil servants, with executive authority for investigation or supervision, tended not only to improve and enlarge their delegated functions but also to be involved in different but related functions, and thus to recommend and obtain an extension of function. With the existence in the public service of officers professionally responsible for the execution of public policy, there was build-up of expertise through the systematic accumulation of evidence and experience, a testing of public policy as laid down by statute, and continuous pressure for the re-formulation, modification, and extension of existing legislation. This process can be seen clearly, for example, in the history of factory legislation, or of the Passenger Acts and their enforcement.[36] There was nothing sinister or planned in such growth; it was the result of the well-intentioned motives of conscientious men to improve and extend "the good work" they were doing; and their expertise, experience and dedication to public duties gave their recommendations scientific

---

[36] For example, see O. MacDonagh, *A Pattern of Government Growth, 1800-60, The Passenger Acts and Their Enforcement* (London: MacGibbon and Kee, 1961).

and moral authority. A similar but more calculating reason for the growth of the public service can be found in W. A. Niskanen's economic theory of bureaucracy.[37] If bureaucrats acted rationally, that is with self-interest, as they did, they acted so as to maximize and continually expand personnel and budgets. Such expansion in any department was a measure of responsibility and status, and of salary, these being all related to the size of a department's budget, the number of its personnel, and the amount of resources it administered. In such a way, E. G. West has clearly demonstrated, the English educational bureaucracy expanded in the nineteenth century.[38] With increasing intervention and the growth of the bureaucracy there was a decline in voluntarism. Public enterprise created a host of classic freerider situations in which it seemed that all benefited and few suffered. Although there was much private exposure of social ills, and much voluntary effort directed at their alleviation or cure, voluntarism was a weak instrument of social reform compared with government enterprise. Parliament had both power and wealth; it was sovereign; its injunctions were legally binding; and it could create and pay for executive authorities. The forward march of government, retrospectively, seems *almost* inevitable; society was caught in a social inquiry trap from which the obvious escape was bureaucratic intervention, and bureaucracies, once created, expanded *almost* autonomously. And the problem is still with us.

## The Intellectuals and the Historians

Have governments become increasingly interventionist, not as a reflex action to the need to solve social problems as suggested above, but as Hayek claims, more because of the influence of the intellectuals, who are predominantly socialists?[39] Hayek defines the intellectuals as "the secondhand dealers in ideas," "neither ... the original thinkers nor ...

---

[37] W. A. Niskanen, *Bureaucracy and Representative Government* (Chicago: Aldine, 1971).

[38] E. G. West, "Educational Slowdown and Public Intervention in 19th-century England: A Study in the Economics of Bureaucracy," *Explorations in Economic History* (New York and London: Academic Press), Vol. XII, No. I, January 1975.

[39] See "The Intellectuals and Socialism," *op. cit.*

the scholar or expert in a particular field" but the "intermediary in the spreading of ideas." This distinction is valid, however, only if it is clearly understood that most of those who claim to be "scholars" and "experts"—most "academics"—are "intellectuals" in Hayek's sense. Defined in this way, the intellectuals' power lies in their ability to shape public opinion. "It is no exaggeration to say," Hayek claims, "that once the more active part of the intellectuals have been converted to a set of beliefs, the process by which these become generally accepted is almost automatic and irresistible."[40] The process of opinion forming by the intellectuals depends on freedom of thought and expression. "The ideal of democracy rests on the belief that the view which will direct government emerges from an independent and spontaneous process."[41] In this process the role of the intellectuals is dominant; they select, translate, and transmit ideas to the general public; they decide "the conventional wisdom" and they propagate it. "The climate of opinion" ("a set of very general preconceptions by which the intellectual judges the importance of new facts and opinions")[42] and "majority opinion" (which, expressed through the ballot box, determines and guides government) are thus the important determinants of public policy. Unfortunately for the health of a free society, however, the intellectuals since the Enlightenment have had "progressive" views; in the eighteenth and nineteenth centuries, democratic and egalitarian views; and in the twentieth century, interventionist and socialist views. In the United States, for example, E. C. Ladd and S. M. Lipset have shown recently that American academics of this century have been predominantly committed to progressive or socialist politics ("liberal" in the modern American sense).[43] In Britain, both the socialist bias of the intellectuals, and their pervasive power, can be seen in the prestige and influence of the Fabian Society and of a large number of distinguished academics who

---

[40] *Ibid.*, pp. 178, 179, 182.
[41] *The Constitution of Liberty*, p. 109.
[42] "The Intellectuals and Socialism," p. 185.
[43] E. C. Ladd and S. M. Lipset, *The Divided Academy* (New York: McGraw Hill, 1975). Sponsored by the Carnegie Commission on Higher Education.

have been publicists for socialism and who have had direct
influence on public policy, for example, the Webbs, the Ham-
monds, Tawney, Cole, Beveridge, Laski, and Titmus.

But why are intellectuals socialists? Initially, almost certainly, to solve social problems. The influence of the eighteenth century idea of progress, with the concomitant view
that social ills are *not* to be endured but are to be identified,
analyzed and cured, led to a preoccupation with social problems coupled with a humane desire for reform. And the
socialists, more than anyone else, offered "an explicit programme of social development, a picture of the kind of future
society at which they were aiming, and a set of general
principles to guide decisions on particular issues."[44] These
principles, moreover, were made operational by the evolution
of the theory of social engineering. "There can be little doubt
that the manner in which during the last hundred years man
has learned to organise the forces of nature has contributed a
great deal towards the creation of the belief that a similar
control of the forces of society would bring compaiable
improvements in human conditions."[45] The possibility of
social engineering made effective "the demand that government should enforce not merely 'formal' but 'substantive'
(i.e., 'distributive' or 'social') justice."[46] This, in particular,
meant the implementation of the most emotionally appealing
and most widely accepted ideal inherited from the eighteenth
century, the ideal of equality. Whereas the liberal view of
society offered the economic anarchy and income inequality
of the free market, the socialist offered the economic order
and social justice of the command economy. The intellectuals
were unwilling to accept "the irrationality" of individualism
and the chaos of real life; they thought that it was possible
"to comprehend social wholes like society," and so they
accepted "a design theory of social institutions."[47] The step
from this point to socialism was easy and natural. Socialism is

---

[44]"The Intellectuals and Socialism," p. 190.

[45]*Ibid.*, p. 187.

[46]*The Constitution of Liberty*, pp. 234-35.

[47]F. A. Hayek, *Individualism and Economic Order* (London: Routledge and
Kegan Paul, 1949), pp. 4, 6.

the opposite of individualism, as are design theories of society. Socialism assumes that "deliberate regulation of all social affairs must necessarily be more successful than the apparently haphazard interplay of independent individuals."[48] When design was attached to inevitability, a package of fatalism and fanaticism was produced. There had to be unquestioning acceptance of socialism. "If the change was to be brought about by the inexorable logic of history, if it was the inevitable result of evolution, there was little need for knowing in detail what exactly the new society would be like."[49] Socialism had become the logical outcome of the process of social evolution.

If socialism was acceptable to the intellectuals because it was scientific, however, allegiance to it was given passion and a large input of moral superiority by the historians of modern capitalism. History "revealed" the horrors of early industrialization under capitalism, and "proved" the exploitation of the working classes. History, in particular, provided the "one supreme myth which more than any other has served to discredit the economic system to which we owe our present-day civilization."[50] This myth was that modern economic growth in capitalist economies was achieved at the expense of the working classes; and the myth was extended to account for all the ills of modern society. The myth is complex in composition, but includes three main beliefs.

> First, the belief that the industrial revolution in England had resulted not only in a deterioration in the standard of living of the mass of the workers for upwards of a century, but also in a permanent deterioration in their way of life; insofar as wealth had increased in the early period, it had resulted only in increasing inequality, with the rich getting richer and the poor poorer. Second, the belief that the subsequent, in-the-long-run improvement in the material condition of the working classes, which the critics of capitalism have found difficult to deny, was caused not by industrialization and economic growth, but by income redistribution, by working class industrial organizations which were able to force a larger share of national income from reluctant capitalists,

---

[48] F. A. Hayek (ed.), *Collectivist Economic Planning* (London: Routledge, 1938), p. 1.

[49] *Ibid.*, p. 13.

[50] *Capitalism and the Historians*, pp. 9-10.

and through the development of the welfare state, which also was the direct result of the increasing political power of the working classes. Third, the belief that much of the increasing wealth of the industrial countries of Europe, which went mainly to the capitalists, came from non-Europeans; increasing European wealth, including that of the masses, was partly at the expense of the non-European masses and was achieved through a process of colonial exploitation known as imperialism.[51]

These beliefs, based on historical myths, have been important in shaping political allegiances. However, little scholarly attention has been given either to the sociology of historical knowledge, or to the pervasive and influential role of history in attitude formation.[52] Perhaps the most useful contribution of *Capitalism and the Historians* was to methodology, and especially to a demonstration of the mix in historical writing of ideology and evidence.[53] History, universally taught at all levels of education and widely read by the general public, should be seen for its potential as an important weapon in ideological conflict. Historical myths about capitalism are basic to the widespread dislike of capitalism, and do much to discredit the economic system of private property and market economy. Destroy these myths, and the easy ideological attack on capitalism is weakened and made more difficult to sustain.

It is a mistake, however, to attribute too much influence to history, which is only one subject at work in opinion-forming which is anti-liberal.[54] Similar attitudes are also propagated in other subjects. Much of the study of literature, for example, has moved from analysis of the universals of artistic expression to the sociology of literature in terms of the author's reaction to relevant social problems. Economics, similarly, is more concerned with the efficiency of intervention, with how

---

[51] R. M. Hartwell, "History and Ideology" (Institute for Humane Studies, *Studies in History and Philosophy*, No. 3, 1974), p. 1. Reprinted from *Modern Age* (Fall, 1974). See, also, the author's unpublished "The Three Great Myths of Modern History."

[52] "History and Ideology," *loc. cit.*

[53] In a perceptive review (*American Economic Review*, 1954), W. T. Easterbrook argued this way, pointing to "the distinction between the evidence of history and the beliefs by which we live."

[54] What follows is a summary of my argument in "History and Ideology," *op. cit.*

to make an interventionist economy work better, than with critical analysis of the interventionist philosophy. Basic to much teaching of economics is the assumption that the market economy is not working because it cannot work, rather than the assumption that market economy does not work because it is not allowed to work. And what schools and universities propagate in formal education, many other institutions reinforce: much of the social teaching of the Christian churches, unfortunately, is interventionist in spirit; the mass media maintain a constant barrage of criticism of liberalism and, in particular, overdramatize the ills of industrial society; creative art caters too often to irresponsible and destructive views of society; both trade unions and employer organizations constantly demand government intervention for vaguely specified, social reasons, and more transient groups like antipollutionists see only government-directed solutions for their problems. It is not surprising, therefore, that so many young people grow up to accept the need for government intervention to solve all society's ills, and to believe that conditions are as bad as they are because of the lack of government intervention.

## Conclusion

"The universal demand for 'conscious' control or direction of social process," writes Hayek, "is one of the most characteristic features of our generation. It expresses perhaps more clearly than any of its other cliches the peculiar spirit of the age."[55] And the growth of government in the democracies is the most important change that has occurred in our generation in the institutional framework of working and living. These are the phenomena for the liberal to explain. If the growth of socialism is seen simply as the supply response to an irresistible demand, or if it is seen simply in supply terms—the autonomous growth of government—the demand has still to be explained. It is important to emphasize that any explanation should take into account both demand and supply factors. Generally concern about socialism by the lib-

---

[55] *The Counter-Revolution of Science*, p. 87.

erals has led to three types of inquiry: analysis of the consequences of socialism (as in Hayek's *The Road to Serfdom*);
definition of the legal and constitutional conditions of liberty
(as in *The Constitution of Liberty*); and explanation of the
anti-capitalist mentality (as in *Capitalism and the Historians*).
Hayek has contributed notably to all these inquiries, but
particularly to the first two. He recognizes the disease, he
knows its consequences, he knows its cure, but he is less
certain about the causes, and he does not know how to
administer the medicine. On the history and development of
the anti-capitalist mentality, nevertheless, Hayek has made
important contributions. Since he argues that the growth of
socialism is to be explained mainly in demand terms, he
identifies the intellectuals (in "The Intellectuals and Socialism") as the decisively important propagandists of socialism,
the operational source of socialist ideology and the main
mechanism for its spread. Hayek also has ideas about why the
intellectuals were converted to socialism. In *The Counter-
Revolution of Science*, for example, he traces the history of
the concept of "social engineering" and explains its attractive-
ness to the intellectual. In a number of writings he explains
how "the design theory of social institutions" and historicism
(based on the idea that "the central aim of all study of
society must be to construct a universal history of mankind,
understood as a scheme of the necessary development of
humanity according to recognizable laws"[56]) have strengthened the intellectuals' convictions that socialism is both desirable and inevitable. In *Capitalism and the Historians*, Hayek
shows that the intellectuals' anti-capitalist mentality is based
largely on an historical myth (that the history of capitalism is
the history of the exploitation of the working classes), an
economic myth (that capitalism is inefficient compared with
socialism), and a moral absolute (that inequality is morally
unacceptable). The combination of ideas, theories and myths
have combined to increase "the desire to give the organized
forces of government greater power to shape social relations
deliberately according to some ideal of social justice."[57] But

[56]*Ibid.*, pp. 196-197.
[57]*The Constitution of Liberty*, p. 235.

this cannot alone explain the growth of government. Not only is the motivation of those who seek socialism, and of those who direct governments, more complex than Hayek generally allows, but as he has often pointed out, there are in society "impersonal and anonymous social processes by which individuals help to create things greater than they know."[58] The many actions of many individuals are moved variously by principle, self-interest, passion and expediency, and the combined social effects are not necessarily beneficial.[59] Even the most respected motives, for example, "the sense of justice and the idea of equality," are based, partly at least, on envy.[60] And the combined consequences of individual actions, whatever their motivation, are difficult, if not impossible, to predict. "By tracing the combined effects of individual actions," Hayek writes, "we discover that many of the institutions on which human achievements have arisen are functioning without a designing or directing mind."[61] Hayek is thinking obviously of an institution like the market which has benefited mankind, but individual actions, even when directed towards the improvement of society,[62] do not necessarily combine beneficially for society. The final and aggregate result, as in the case of social inquiry, is often larger than, and much different from, that intended by the individuals who initiated action. It is important to remember that "the invisible hand" is not always beneficent, and the liberal must accept that reality.

---

[58] *Individualism and Economic Order*, p. 6.

[59] In a recent book M. Cowling (*The Impact of Hitler: British Politics and British Policy 1933-1940*, Cambridge University Press, 1975) has pointed to the "implied contradiction between expediency and principle" in the "rational" actions of politicians. "Rational" here means what politicians can understand. It means working through contingency and accident, not rising above them. It means that principles are manifestations of personality no less than interests and passions and that all three form the context of political consciousness."

[60] H. Schoeck, *Envy. A Theory of Social Behaviour* (London: Secker and Warburg, English Edition, 1969), Ch. 14.

[61] *Individualism and Economic Order*, p. 7.

[62] Read, for example, the fascinating volume of J. Passmore, *The Perfectability of Man* (London: Duckworth, 1970), an ironic and critical account of 3,000 years of a utopian quest for the improvement of man.

# William F. Buckley, Jr.

# The Road to Serfdom: The Intellectuals and Socialism

As we look back on the excitement caused by the publication of Friedrich Hayek's *The Road to Serfdom*, we wonder how it could have happened. It is a tribute to him, and to his small book, that we should be able to say this. The principal theses of the book are by now so very well known, even if they are not by any means universally accepted, that they appear almost self-evident. Hayek has always taken scrupulous care to give credit, if it is faintly plausible to do so, to others who articulated ideas before he did, and indeed sometimes, on reading the footnotes to *The Constitution of Liberty*, one almost has the feeling that the book is a collection of after-dinner toasts by Hayek to great philosophers, political thinkers, and economists, from Thales to Ludwig von Mises. But he cannot shrug off the credit for having brought much of it all together: the integrated perception of the relation between law, and justice, and liberty. And, in an age swooning with passion for a centralized direction of social happiness and economic plenitude, that squirt of ice water, presaged by the quotation he selected as epigraph to his book, the wry observation of David Hume that "it is seldom that liberty of any kind is lost all at once." Rather, Hayek explained, it is lost gradually; and it is lost by assigning vague, extra-lawful mandates to men of political authority who take on tasks which they cannot be expected to perform without absorbing all the knowledge, values, preferences, and passions of all their fellow men; and this no political authority—indeed, no animate or inanimate body—can do. Accordingly, the political authority has no alternative but to usurp. The necessary result of that usurpation is the corresponding loss in

the freedom of the body in which the authority previously
reposed. Over a period of time, that kind of movement must
lead us down the road to serfdom, into that amnestic void
toward which, Orwell intuited, evil men were for evil purposes
expressly bent on taking us; which void Professor Oakeshott
sees us headed toward under the impulse of our own indis-
position to bear the heavy responsibilities of freedom.

Hayek brought to his thesis the great prestige of an
economist unblemished by the tattoo of ideology. Indeed,
during the 1930s his reputation was almost exclusively technical, and we are informed that historians will in due course
remark that the great technical debate of the early 1930s was
actually between Hayek and Keynes. One can only hope that
by the time they get around to saying this, they will get
around to saying that Hayek won. Now that the Nobel Prize
Committee has taken pains to honor Professor Hayek's technical contributions to economic science, alongside Gunnar
Myrdal's contributions to something or other, one is reminded
of a sentence from Hayek's *Intellectuals and Socialism*:

> It is especially significant for our problem that every scholar can
> probably name several instances from his field of men who have
> undeservedly achieved a popular reputation as great scientists
> solely because they hold what the intellectuals regard as "progres-
> sive" political views; but I have yet to come across a single
> instance where such a scientific pseudo-reputation has been
> bestowed for political reasons on a scholar of more conservative
> leanings.

Hayek brought then a great prestige and a dazzling capacity
for synthesis to propositions which, although they had been
ably defended over a period of years, were widely thought, by
the academic community in particular, to constitute nothing
much weightier than the ululations of a propertied class
suddenly bereft—in virtue of its incompetence to handle a
great depression, and its forfeited authority over public
opinion—of power. To hear such thoughts uttered by businessmen at conventions of the National Association of Manufacturers, and quoted in the *Reader's Digest*, was one thing. To
hear them uttered by a quiet, profound academician, and
reprinted in the *Reader's Digest*, was something else. The
counterattack was vigorous, in some cases highly personal and

vindictive, in other instances grand and supercilious. But before long Hayek was writing that the "hot socialism," as he called it, against which he had polemicized in *The Road to Serfdom*, was doctrinally dead, but that its "conceptions" had penetrated so deeply into the public consciousness that it mattered not very much that the theology of socialism was discredited, any more than it appears to matter greatly that, if we take Solzhenitsyn's word for it—and I will; today, tomorrow, and always—one cannot find in all of Moscow an orthodox Marxist. The forms of socialism are quite sufficient to do the deadly work. The intellectuals, many of them all along uneasy about the chimerical vanities of utopian socialism, are no less entrenched in their distaste for the kind of society they understand to be the necessary consequence of a free market economy. That passion for freedom that catapulted us two hundred years ago into national independence and into the most exciting attempt in history at the incorporation of human freedom into a federal constitution, had by and large been reduced to a velleity for some kinds of freedom, though a complicated libertarian vocabulary was constructed, the purpose of which was to demonstrate that freedom is in fact enhanced, rather than diminished, when we assign to the government control over our lives.

Irving Kristol has said that the stunning paradox is that the intellectual fight against socialism is triumphant even as the forces of socialism triumph: and that this they manage to do by arguing that socialism isn't really about economic efficiency and, correlatively, by disdaining freedom insofar as it attaches in any way to property or commerce. We are several times disadvantaged in the struggle. For one thing, the arguments of the collectivists are more obviously appealing. For another, "it seems to be true," as Hayek wistfully put it in his essay on the subject, "that it is on the whole the more active, intelligent and original men among the intellectuals who most frequently incline toward socialism, while its opponents are often of an inferior caliber." And, finally, though the other side is increasingly evasive on the point, you can spot, slouching about in the grander statements of socialist purpose, inflections of an eschatological character; which,

in the nature of things, traditional liberalism lacks, quite
properly so. Yet even if we eschew a redemptive creed we
should, Hayek says, "offer a new liberal program which
appeals to the imagination." In fact, he goes further, as we
shall see.

I elect to touch on these three observations of Hayek,
taking the liberty of treating his essay on the intellectuals as
something of an afterword to *The Road to Serfdom*, which it
properly is, I think. I advance three propositions.

*The freedom to deceive is overindulged.*

In one of her excellent essays, Simone Weil remarked that
Jacques Maritain's account of the history of ancient Greece was
factually incorrect in respect of the life of the helots, and
that in a just and well-ordered world his book would be
suppressed, and he would himself be subject to a civil lawsuit,
the plaintiff being the Truth, which, in Simone Weil's society,
would have legal standing.

Now this position is something of a caricature, but it is
crankily instructive in an age where freedom of expression has
brought virtual immunity to those who deceive. Foremost
among those who do so, as a class, are, of course, the
politicians. But in a society in which there is also freedom to
criticize, the politicians would probably not get away with it
except for the indulgence of the only class of citizens professionally trained to isolate untruth, and shoot it, bang bang,
right down to earth.

I do not seek to codify this proposition by giving it
constitutional lineaments, or even by proclaiming a Hillsdale
Manifesto. But I do propose that we meditate far more
extensively and seriously than we have done since the publication of *The Road to Serfdom* the civil consequences of the
extraordinary immunity of the advocates of the superstitions
of communism, of socialism, of redistributionism, of inflation,
of *dirigisme*, from the bar of critical opinion. It has been
remarked that Professor Hayek's public manners are exem-
plary. Nowhere in the literature does he give way to spite,
nowhere—quite the contrary—does he suggest that there are
ulterior motives in those who, piping us down the road to
serfdom, make the music of abundance and justice and joy. It

is perhaps the most frequently summoned jape at the expense
of representative democracy to recount the story of the
earnest legislator who sought one day to lighten the load of
the schoolchildren of Indiana by introducing a law that would
trim down the value of *pi* from 3.1416, to the more manage-
able figure of 3. The response was instantaneous. It did not
come alone from men and women professionally capable of
handling calculus. The hilarity came alike from the mathe-
maticians and their fellow travelers, whose derisory laughter is
even now renewed with each retelling of the famous episode.

I shall return this afternoon to the nervous center of the
cultured world, New York City, which groans under the weight
of the greatest density of intellectuals per acre this side of
Socrates' academy; but I have not heard it asserted from any
New Yorker, save the isolated immigrants from Mont Pelerin,
that no respectable canon of redistributive justice recognizes the
duty of residents of Detroit, or West Virginia, or Key West—
or even Palo Alto—to subsidize the cost of rapid transit in
New York City. Much there is that we do not know, but
some things there are that we do know. And self-respect
requires that we stimulate the social and academic sanction
against that which is misleading, let alone preposterous. But
Ralph Nader, the only social hero of our time, is obsessed by
how many corn flakes are missing from the package sold at
the grocery store, while undisturbed by how many middles
are undistributed in the speech of a typical politician of the
left. The social success of freedom requires something of an
extra-ideological devotion to analytical rigor and to the integrity of language. Hayek quotes Dorothy Fosdick in a state of
what one can only describe as despair, upon reading John
Dewey on the meaning of freedom. "The stage ... is fully
set," she writes, "for ... [the identification of liberty with
some other principle, such as equality] only when the definitions of liberty and of equality have been so juggled that
both refer to approximately the same condition of activity.
An extreme example of such sleight of hand is provided by
John Dewey when he says: *'If Freedom is combined with a
reasonable amount of equality, and security is taken to mean
cultural and moral security and also material safety, I do not*

*think that security is compatible with anything but freedom.'*
After redefining two concepts so that they mean approxi-
mately the same condition of activity," Miss Fosdick sighs,
Dewey "assures us that the two are compatible."

As the intellectual case against socialism becomes, by experience and analysis, firmer, the threat of socialism becomes,
paradoxically, greater; and I find myself wondering whether
the soupy indulgence shown by right-minded intellectuals to
those who deceive in order to play out their ideological
passions, does not emerge less as an act of intellectual charity
than of moral despair and epistemological pessimism.

*The inferiority of the class of intellectual defenders of
capitalism is less critical a factor in contemporary circumstances than the moral inferiority of capitalists.*

Hayek has complained about the "inferior caliber" of those
intellectuals who incline in favor of the free market, by
comparison with those who defend socialism. He is right,
though less so, by far, than when he wrote those dismaying
words, before the great intellectual offensive of the past 20
years, for which he is so substantially responsible, which has
left the socialists in disarray. Professor John Kenneth Galbraith, giving an interview recently to a London journalist,
said that he was forced to admit that, whereas 15 years ago
he and his colleagues were pretty well convinced that there
were no serious problems left unanswered in economics, he
recognizes now how much there is left to discover.

If there is so much left for you to discover, *a fortiori* we
can imagine how much there is left for Professor Galbraith to
discover. One wishes, discreetly, that, as one experiences one's
ignorance, *pari passu* one would lower one's voice. But to be
apodictic is of course a necessary part of Professor Galbraith's
style. I was recently with him in Switzerland attempting, at
lunch, to find a common blank in our calendars, in order to
schedule a network exchange in New York for which we had
contracted. I proposed to him the first week in April, but he
replied, studying his engagement book, that that would not
do, that in the first week in April he would be lecturing at
the University of Moscow. "Oh?" I said. "What do you have
left to teach them?" So long as Galbraith continues to teach

economics to the Soviet Union, we will have a market for our excess grain. His contribution to the Ever Normal Granary.

For all of his tergiversations, Galbraith has never wavered on one inclination, and that is his contempt for American capitalists—I speak, here and below, of the class, not of individuals. I fear that in this matter he is uniquely correct. He chronicles not only the cupidity, but the parasitic habits of so many of them, the predatory character of their belief in the marketplace. I hope to be understood as saying something more interesting than that greed is the root of many evils, a bipartisan conclusion about human nature. Although Adam Smith did not use the word to describe the instinct of industrial man to improve his lot, he was sardonically aware of the factor of inordinate self-interest, and of the sublimated variations one could play on it. He wrote, for instance, in *The Wealth Of Nations* that "the late resolution of the Quakers in Pennsylvania to set at liberty all their Negro slaves, may satisfy us that their number cannot be very great."

Recently, addressing the AFL-CIO in Washington, Solzhenitsyn proclaimed the natural alliance of the American worker and the Russian worker in an entirely non-Marxist frame. But, he added, there is "another alliance: the alliance between our Communist leaders and your capitalists." He went on to discuss a recent exhibit in the Soviet Union of the United States anti-criminal technology that engrossed the Russians, who instantly put in orders for the lot, cash on the barrelhead. The problem, Solzhenitsyn pointed out—breaking loose from the disinterested terms of the marketplace—being that we were selling our scientific paraphernalia not to the law-abiding for use against criminals, but to criminals for use against the law-abiding: rather like inventing the guillotine for the purpose of slaughtering cattle, and then selling it to Robespierre in full knowledge of the uses to which he intended to put it.

"This is something which is almost incomprehensible to the human mind," Solzhenitsyn said: "that burning greed for profit which goes beyond all reason, all self-control, all conscience— only to get money." Solzhenitsyn cannot be expected to be familiar with the nuances by which a successfully ordered free market economy administrates, and finally puts a limit on, the uses of greed. But we can hardly blame him if he sees, with that laser purity of his moral vision, only the silhouettes: American businessmen, like their great-grandfathers trading in the slave market, anxious to turn a profit by trafficking with the contemporary generation of slavemasters.

But that greed, which so outraged such resonant critics of the free market as Veblen and Tawney, is less I think a mutation of capitalism, let alone an organic development of it, than a culturally conditioned indifference to principle, a stubborn moral nescience, a fugitive unconcern for cultivation of values only a painstaking care for which can guarantee the survival of free men. I speak of a class of self-conscious men, atrophied by two generations of contempt by academicians and moralists, which reacts by exhibiting a libertine indifference to the quality or direction of the political-economic instruction in the colleges they patronize; to which they send their sons and daughters, for impacted indoctrination in the evils of the society they sustain, or are sustained by. Of a class that—out of cultivated ignorance—permitted Ludwig von Mises and even Hayek to live in an economic insecurity very nearly paralyzing; that sustains, indeed causes to flourish through gaudy advertising, the popular journals that combine, in resolutely fixed ratio, licentious assaults on the venerable, delicately-nurtured restraints on rampant biological appetites, and fundamentalist condemnations of American institutions and ideals. The American capitalist whose image reifies in the mind of the young is not even the smug, canny, willful powerbroker of Upton Sinclair. He is the inarticulate, self-conscious, bumbling mechanic of the private sector, struck dumb by the least cliché of socialism, fleeing into the protective arms of government at the least hint of commercial difficulty, delighting secretly in the convenient power of the labor union to negotiate for an entire industry, uniformly successful only in his escapist ambition to grow duller and duller as the years go by, eyes left, beseeching popular favor. Poor Miss Rand sought to give him a massive dose of testosterone, to make him virile and irresistible, leader of a tri-

umphant meritocratic revolt against asphyxiative government
... but soon it transpired, even as Russell Kirk predicted, that
her novels were being read not because of their jackbooted
individualism, but because of the fornicating bits.

The entrepreneurial class can only change its image by
taking lusty joy from its achievements, and by seeing it, as
Isabel Paterson insisted we must see it—whole or not at all—as
springing season after season from a trampoline of assumptions which are the warp and woof of freedom and progress. I
shall not soon forget the scene, symbolic of the triumphs of
demogogic terror over productive enterprise: Senator Scoop
Jackson, sitting high in his committee chair, addressing the
12 top officials of the oil and gas industry meekly astride
their stools at the bar of justice, publicly chastising them on
their obscene profits. How bracing it would have been if, as
one man, they had risen to their feet early in the tirade and
walked out, leaving the senator lecturing only to the television
cameras, which of course he was primarily addressing. Cecil B.
DeMille gave up a million dollar contract because he refused
to pay the sum of one dollar to a labor union with a closed
shop. Cecil B. DeMille is dead, and all the mighty work of
Hayek, and Mises, and Friedman have not bred his replacement.

*The opposition to socialism must remain primarily negative,*
*and takes strength from being so.*

Hayek, in the passage already quoted about the need for
new liberal programs that appeal to the imagination, goes on.
"We must," he says, "make the building of a free society
once more an intellectual adventure, a deed of courage. What
we lack is a liberal utopia, a program which seems neither a
mere defense of things as they are nor a diluted kind of
socialism, but a truly liberal radicalism which does not spare
the susceptibilities of the mighty. . . . "

Hayek is so very correct in so much of what he says, one
hesitates to cavil, and does so only under the libertine dispen-
sation of this permissive organization.

Of *course* we need imagination: so does BBD&O in selling
hot dogs or shampoo.

Certainly we need courage, a quality of Evel Knievel as of

Thomas More, with, however, a world's discrimination between their use of it, though I do not need to be reminded
that Knievel has survived, and More did not.

Intellectual adventure is nowadays best defined as treating
respectfully that which was accepted as a truism only a few
generations ago.

The need for a liberal radicalism is manifest, and no single
person living has contributed more than Hayek to an intima-
tion of what such radicalism might bring us by, for instance, a
separation of the legislature into two bodies, the one authorized only to pass laws of the kind associated with the rule of
law, laws generic, impartial, intelligible; the structural beams
on which the folkways of society weave about like ivy,
susceptible to training, direction, fancy, caprice even.

What we do *not* need is anything that suggests that human
freedom is going to lead us to utopia. For one thing, it isn't
going to; and therefore any conceits on the matter are quickly
seen as ideological vanity, discrediting to the unassuming virtues, however exhilarating when discreetly imputed to human
freedom.

Hayek is so cautious a craftsman as to cause even someone
intoxicated by his summons to intellectual adventure to wonder whether his summons to utopia might have been the
mischievous working of atmospheric gravity on his numinous
pen. My knowledge of his work is limited to his nontechnical
writings and flawed by my porous memory, but I cannot
offhand remember any other call by him to the pursuit of
utopia—which is not even listed as a subject heading in *The
Constitution of Liberty*—nor even of utopia's poor relation,
eudaemonia, though I am buoyant enough to believe that if
we were to follow Hayek's prescriptions, we would come, if
not to eudaemonia, at least to something not far removed
from that happiness which results from the governance of
reason, always understanding that that is an incomplete, indeed a contingent, happiness.

The perspectives of Hayek are not only great, every re-
corded intellectual endeavor serving him as a stilt of great
cumulative elevation. They are so great as to induce him to
deliberate respectfully the relativist obsessions of other

thinkers, which I however view as lime spread over Hayek's life's work. Thus he quotes Michael Polanyi as saying a few years after *The Road to Serfdom* was published,

> The conceptions by the light of which men will judge our own ideas in a thousand years—or perhaps even in fifty years—are beyond our guess. If a library of the year 3000 came into our hands today, we could not understand its contents. How should we consciously determine a future which is, by its very nature, beyond our comprehension? Such presumption reveals only the narrowness of an outlook uninformed by humility.

In his own words, Hayek declares:

> it would be an error to believe that, to achieve a higher civilization, we have merely to put into effect the ideas now guiding us. If we are to advance, we must leave room for a continuous revision of our present conceptions and ideals which will be necessitated by further experience.

I find it perplexing to combine this high relativism with any notion, however careless, of utopia. And although fashionable rhetoric flirts alike with the elasticity of standards (*what is freedom?*) and with the realizability of utopia on earth, I find the temptation to the latter illusion less frequent in the work of serious conservatives, or even of dress-suited Whigs, than in that of the ideologists who have done so much to wreck our century.

Hayek gave an example of his great intellectual courage when, in his great book on liberty, he girded his loins, kissed good-bye to his wife, made out his will, and came out against the progressive income tax. That was both audacious and exhilarating; and indeed if ever his counsel on the matter were accepted, I have no doubt whatever that any society would benefit comprehensively, and that the tuning fork of justice would resonate with the joy of bells in the morning. But we would not have achieved utopia. We would be left, for instance, without any guide to how the liberated taxpayer would spend his repatriated surplus; I know of nothing in libertarian literature that is instructive on the point. There is a great and brooding literature that is instructive on such moral matters, but it is a literature that speaks with a humility that goes far, far beyond the historicistic humility of Michael Polanyi in reminding us that heaven is not for this, but for another, world, and that final satisfactions are taken from adventures in faith, hope, and charity unrelated to the marketplace. In that other world, I do not hesitate to predict, Friedrich von Hayek will be garlanded and praised for his contributions to a social philosophy that reflects the dignity of metaphysical man. If I should happen to make it there, I shall gladly join as a minor member of the chorus, confident that the final act of utopianization will bring my voice into total harmony with those of the legions who praise his name.

Gottfried Dietze

# Hayek on
# the Rule
# of Law

## Introduction

Favoring the freedom of the individual, modern liberalism came about as a reaction to the despotism of *ancien régimes*, to excessive governmental controls and regulations. These threats to liberty did not disappear in the democratic era. During the past decades, liberals have emphasized how big government, in a large measure a result of socialism and the welfare state, has posed a serious challenge to freedom.

In recent years, this concern has been complemented by a fear of anarchy. Everywhere, liberal nations are beset by riots and crime. While the idea of the rule of law continues to mean the safety of the individual from big government, it also has come to imply the need for a government that is strong enough to protect individuals from illegal attacks by their fellow men.

A time in which the very existence of liberal society is in jeopardy suggests an examination of how great liberals have felt about the law. In a conference dedicated to the work of F. A. von Hayek, a study of his remarks on the rule of law over the past thirty years—the period in which he emerged as a social philosopher—seems to be appropriate.

## Liberty and the Rule of Law

Freedom is the predominant value in Hayek's social thought.[1]

---

[1] Hayek uses the words "liberty" and "freedom" interchangeably, a practice followed throughout this paper. To Hayek, there does not seem to exist any accepted distinction in meaning between them, although he has a personal preference for the latter. *The Constitution of Liberty* (London, 1960), pp. 11, 421 n. 1.

107

Adenauer, whom de Madariaga called "the only living
statesman of world-format,"[2] and who, together with Ludwig
Erhard, brought about the recovery of West Germany, once
stated that "one must look at things so deeply as to make
them simple. If one remains at the surface of things only,
they are not simple. However, if one looks into the depth,
one sees what is real, and that always is simple."[3] No matter
how deeply we study Hayek's work of the past decades, we
always are aware of the simple fact that it really turns around
the pursuit of liberty.

Aside from calling himself "simply an unrepentant Old
Whig,"[4] Hayek also indicates that he is a "mere scholar."[5] In
the clear style desirable for scholarship that is evident in
Hayek's writing, the idea of freedom is obvious; it can be
noted in the titles of his books. Since a road to something
can only be a road away from its opposite, the title, "The
Road to Serfdom," immediately indicates that the author is
describing only the road away from freedom. Even more
obvious is the message conveyed by the words "The Constitution of Liberty." Whether one sees behind these words a
specific constitution such as, for instance, the constitution of
the United States (to which Hayek, however, refers as "a
constitution of liberty"[6]), or the process of constituting or
establishing liberty, or a state of fitness (which Hayek later
said he had in mind[7]), there can be no doubt about the
central position of liberty. The same is true of the title,
"Law, Legislation and Liberty." Two means—law and legislation—precede the end, liberty, with one generally aiding, and
the other challenging liberty.

The dominance of freedom in Hayek's philosophy has been
widely recognized. The author of *The Road to Serfdom* has

---

[2] Salvador de Madariaga, "Die deutschen Wahlen in weltpolitischer Sicht,"
leading article in *Neue Zürcher Zeitung*, Sept. 1, 1957.

[3] This statement by Konrad Adenauer is the motto of Anneliese Poppinga,
*Konrad Adenauer* (Stuttgart, 1975), p. 5.

[4] *The Constitution of Liberty*, p. 409.

[5] *Law, Legislation and Liberty*, Vol. I, *Rules and Order* (Chicago, 1973), p. 4.

[6] *The Constitution of Liberty*, pp. 178-182.

[7] *Rules and Order*, p. 3.

been compared to John Stuart Mill.[8] Mill's essay on liberty
was published about the middle of the last century, a century
that has been called the English as well as the liberal century.[9] That work reflects an existing general acceptance of,
and confidence in, freedom. Hayek's *The Road to Serfdom*,
on the other hand, was brought out when liberty had become
discredited some four score years later by "the socialists of all
parties" to whom the book is especially addressed.[10] The work
laments the trend toward a general decline of freedom in the
midst of socialist and Keynesian economics.[11] In a similar
comparison to Mill, *The Constitution of Liberty* was praised
as "the twentieth-century successor to John Stuart Mill's
essay 'On Liberty'."[12] Also, the first volume of *Law, Legislation and Liberty*, entitled *Rules and Order*, can be considered a work written for the sake of freedom.[13]

Hayek himself has made it clear that he considers the
protection of liberty the purpose of his work. *The Road to
Serfdom*, Hayek confesses in its preface, is a political book,
written for "certain ultimate values." The quotations on the
title page leave no doubt as to which one among these values
he considers the most important. "It is seldom that liberty of
any kind is lost all at once," Hayek quotes David Hume, and

---

[8] For an attack on that book, see Herman Finer, *Road to Reaction* (Boston, 1946).

[9] See Karl Heinz Pfeffer, *England: Vormacht der bürgerlichen Welt* (Hamburg, 1940). England as the motherland of liberalism, the country with a liberal tradition, has frequently been pointed out by Hayek. For instance, in *The Road to Serfdom* (London, 1944), p. 54 n.; "Entstehung und Verfall des Rechtsstaatsi-
deales," in Albert Hunold, ed., *Wirtschaft ohne Wunder* (Zürich, 1953), pp. 33-46; *The Constitution of Liberty*, pp. 162-175; "The Legal and Political Philosophy of David Hume," in *Studies in Philosophy, Politics and Economics* (Chicago, 1967), pp. 106-108; *Rules and Order*, pp. 84-85.

[10] *The Road to Serfdom*, p. iv.

[11] According to John Chamberlain's article in *The Wall Street Journal*, Oct. 24, 1974, p. 18, on occasion of the award of the Nobel Prize to Hayek, Hayek at the founding of the Mont Pelerin Society was prevailed upon by Leonard E. Read not to name the society "John Stuart Mill Society" because of Mill's flirt with socialism in his later work. In his last work Hayek denounces "totalitarian doctrines, of which socialism is merely the noblest and most influential." *Rules and Order*, p. 6.

[12] Henry Hazlitt, *Newsweek*, February 15, 1960.

[13] This paper went to press before the publication of the second and third volumes of *Law, Legislation and Liberty*.

adds a word by de Tocqueville: "I should have loved freedom, I believe, at all times, but in the time in which we live I am ready to worship it." In *The Constitution of Liberty*, his aim is "to picture an ideal, to show how it can be achieved, and to explain what its realization would mean in practice." Clearly, that ideal is freedom. *The Constitution of Liberty* is a sequel to *The Road to Serfdom*, starting out, as it does, by quoting Pericles asking about "the road by which we reached our position," a position characterized by the fact that the "freedom which we enjoy in our government extends also to our ordinary life." It is telling that Hayek trimmed the words of Pericles in a way that makes the idea of freedom stand out in the center, shielded by sentences that stress the value of the laws as if he wanted to emphasize the central position of liberty. He writes that "freedom under the law ... is the chief concern of this book." Significantly, *The Constitution of Liberty* closes with two references to Adam Smith, the last of which speaks of the "general principles which are always the same." Hayek, confessing to belong to the party of liberty, admits of no doubt that these principles are those of freedom.[14] Just as *The Constitution of Liberty* is meant to be a sequel to *The Road to Serfdom, Law, Legislation and Liberty* is a continuation and elaboration of *The Constitution of Liberty*. Hayek writes: "If I had known when I published *The Constitution of Liberty* that I should proceed to the task attempted in the present work, I should have reserved that title for it."[15] *Law, Legislation and Liberty*, which suggests constitutional arrangements conducive to a maximal realization of freedom principles in concrete societies, is the practical complement to the more theoretical *The Constitution of Liberty*.

In an article on the causes of the permanent threat to freedom, published a year after *The Constitution of Liberty*, Hayek hastens to complement his defense of liberty in that book, as if he wanted to make doubly sure of the protection of freedom. He writes: "An effective defense of liberty must

---

[14] *The Constitution of Liberty*, pp. vii, 1, 153, 411.
[15] *Rules and Order*, p. 3.

... of necessity be inflexible, dogmatic and doctrinaire and must not make concessions to considerations of expediency. The quest for freedom can be successful only if it is considered a general principle of political morality, the application of which in the concrete case does not need a justification." Toward the end of that article, he goes so far as to state that "liberty is not just one value among others, a maxim of morality on a par with all other maxims, but the source of, and necessary condition for, all other individual values." This marks a significant change from a draft for an introduction to a planned German edition of *The Constitution of Liberty*, also mentioned in that article, stating that "liberty is not only one value among many values, but the source of, and condition for, most other values." Liberty is no longer considered the source and prerequisite of *most* other values, but of *all* other values.[16]

In *Rules and Order*, Hayek repeats this attitude: "A successful defence of freedom must ... be dogmatic and make no concessions to expediency, even where it is not possible to show that, besides the known beneficial effects, some particular harmful result would also follow from its infringement. Freedom will prevail only if it is accepted as a general principle whose application to particular instances requires no justification. It is thus a misunderstanding to blame classical liberalism for having been too doctrinaire. Its defect was not that it adhered too stubbornly to principles, but rather that it lacked principles sufficiently definite to provide clear guidance...." Quoting Strabo, Hayek writes that "liberty is a state's highest good."[17]

The unquestionable predominance of freedom in Hayek's scale of values, however, cannot obscure the fact that to him, liberty is under law and exists according to the laws.

True, Hayek indicates that there is an intangible, all-embracing general freedom that is not under the law, a freedom of which only parts are defined by, and thus under, the

---

[16]"Die Ursachen der ständigen Gefährdung der Freiheit," in Franz Böhm, Friedrich A. Lutz, Fritz W. Meyer, eds., *Ordo*, XII (1961), pp. 105, 107-109.

[17]*Rules and Order*, pp. 61, 94. On page 57 he writes that "freedom can be preserved only if it is treated as a supreme principle."

law. This indication cannot be seen in his distinction between
"liberty" and "liberties," for he considers both to be under
the law.[18] It follows from other statements he makes. He
quotes Lincoln, for example, saying that the world has never
had a good definition of the word liberty; he refers to
Montesquieu's famous passage about the many things men
have understood under liberty; and he cites other authors who
could not agree on what freedom is.[19] This mystery that
surrounds freedom undefined by law proves its existence,
which is further indicated by the fact that to Hayek, the
"state of liberty or freedom" (he has in mind liberty or
freedom under law) is "that condition of men in which
coercion of some by others is reduced as much as possible in
society."[20] Hayek thus acknowledges that his kind of freedom is something relative, existing as much as possible in a
society. Thus he implies that there must be a freedom that
is more absolute and more comprehensive than the one
existing in society. Since freedom in society is freedom according to the law of that society, that is, defined by that law,
there must be an undefined, meta-legal freedom which, in
view of the fact that law by definition restricts,[21] must be

---

[18] *The Constitution of Liberty*, pp. 11-21.

[19] *Ibid.*, pp. 11-21, 421-425.

[20] *Ibid.*, p. 11.

[21] To Hayek, who writes of those for whom law and liberty are irreconcilable
(*Rules and Order*, p. 52), the restriction of freedom by law is most evident in the
formalistic concept of the *Rechtsstaat* ("Entstehung und Verfall des Rechtsstaatsideales," pp. 57-65), in government intervention (*The Constitution of Liberty*, pp. 220-223), in legislation (*Rules and Order*, pp. 124-144). It is not so
much evident in the gradually grown law, which he also refers to as "*the law*,"
or "the lawyer's law" (see n. 73). Although he considers that law "the law of
liberty" (*The Constitution of Liberty*, p. 205), "the chief protection of the
freedom of the individual" (*Rules and Order*, p. 67), and although he believes with
Cicero "that we obey the law in order to be free" (*The Constitution of Liberty*, p.
166) and subscribes to the "great tradition" according to which "law and liberty
could not exist apart from each other" (*Rules and Order*, p. 52), nevertheless he
leaves no doubt that the gradually grown law also restricts liberty. That law
constitutes not only "a limitation on the powers of all government" (*The Constitution of Liberty*, p. 205), but also a limitation on the freedom of the individual.
The thesis of *Law and Order* is to favor "a condition of liberty in which all are
allowed to use their knowledge for their purposes, restrained only by rules of just
conduct of universal application," that is, restrained by the law. That law is law
"in the sense of enforced rules of conduct." (*Rules and Order*, pp. 55, 72).

less restricted than the freedom under law. Furthermore, Hayek writes that "the quest for individual freedom in the last analysis is due to the recognition of the inevitable limitation of our knowledge."[22] Inevitable human limitations limit man's knowledge, including his knowledge of liberty. They result in a continuous quest for more and more definitions by the law of the known parts of the general, all-embracing, meta-legal[23] freedom.

Despite all these indications that he sees a freedom broader than the one existing under law, Hayek, who asserts that "man never existed without laws,"[24] emphasizes that the freedom he has in mind ("a state in which each can use his knowledge for his purposes,"[25]) is one under law. This is evident in his quotation of Pericles. He refers to Cicero's *omnes legum servi sumus ut liberi esse possumus.*[26] He approves of Locke's making it clear that there can be no liberty without law, quoting him at some length in *The Constitution of Liberty.*[27] He is glad that Montesquieu "represented a government of law as the essence of liberty"[28] and that Voltaire believed in freedom under law.[29] He elaborates

---

[22]"Die Ursachen der ständigen Gefährdung der Freiheit," p. 103.

[23]For Hayek's ideas on the meta-legal doctrine, compare *The Constitution of Liberty*, pp. 205-207; *Rules and Order*, pp. 134-135. As early as 1953 Hayek mentioned "meta-juristic criteria." ("Entstehung und Verfall des Rechtsstaatsideales," p. 60.)

[24]"Arten der Ordnung," *Ordo*, XIV (1963), pp. 10-11.

[25]*Rules and Order*, pp. 55-56.

[26]*The Constitution of Liberty*, p. 462 n. 36.

[27]As an introductory motto to the chapter, "The Origins of the Rule of Law" he quotes Locke: "The end of the law is, not to abolish or restrain, but to preserve and enlarge freedom. For in all the states of created beings capable of laws, where there is no law there is no freedom. For liberty is to be free from restraint and violence from others; which cannot be where there is no law: and is not, as we are told, a liberty for every man to do what he lists. (For who could be free when every other man's humour might domineer over him?) But a liberty to dispose, and order as he lists, his person, actions, possessions, and his whole property, within the allowance of those laws under which he is, and therein not to be the subject of the arbitrary will of another, but freely follow his own." *The Constitution of Liberty*, p. 162. See also *The Road to Serfdom*, p. 62 n. 1.

[28]*The Constitution of Liberty*, p. 194. Earlier, Hayek had quoted Montesquieu's statement, "nous sommes donc libre, parce que nous vivons sous les lois civiles." "Entstehung und Verfall des Rechtsstaatsideales." p. 47.

[29]*The Road to Serfdom*, p. 61.

Hume's concept of freedom under law in an article.[30] He praises the American constitution as "a constitution of liberty," a law constituting and protecting liberty.[31] With approval, he quotes Kant: "Man is free if he needs to obey no person but solely the laws."[32] He writes in so many words that freedom is "always freedom under the law."[33]

If freedom is under the law, one could conclude that it is inferior to the law. This, however, is contrary to Hayek's opinion. While freedom is under the law, the law is not superior to freedom. The formal subordination of liberty under the law does not affect the material subordination of the law to liberty. For law is merely a means which has the protection of freedom as its end. Law serves a purpose. In *The Constitution of Liberty*, Hayek writes that the general rules of law were intended to protect the private sphere.[34] In *Rules and Order*, he devotes a whole sub-chapter to "the 'purpose' of law." His now putting the word "purpose" into quotation marks does not mean that he no longer believes that law is a means to an end. It either implies emphasis on the fact that law has a purpose, or on the fact that Hayek wants to point to different concepts of the purpose of the law. He cites a great deal of ambiguity and confusion about the purpose of the law, from Kant's emphasis on the purposelessness of the rules of just conduct to the utilitarians from Bentham to Jhering, who regard purpose as the central feature of the law. Nevertheless, he leaves no doubt that if purpose refers to concrete foreseeable results of particular actions, then the particularistic utilitarianism of Bentham is wrong; if purpose means aiming at an abstract order the particular contents of which are unpredictable, then Kant's denial is not justified. He approves of Hume's emphasis upon the function of law as a whole irrespective of the particular effects.[35] When he writes that "*an abstract order can be the aim of the*

---

[30]"The Legal and Political Philosophy of David Hume."

[31]*The Constitution of Liberty*, pp. 178-182.

[32]*The Road to Serfdom*, p. 61.

[33]"Die Ursachen der ständigen Gefährdung der Freiheit," p. 107.

[34]*The Constitution of Liberty*, p. 220.

[35]*Rules and Order*, pp. 112-113.

*rules of conduct,*"[36] he makes it clear that law is a means to an end. That end is not only the enforcement of legal norms—another proof that Hayek considers law a means to an end[37]—but also the promotion of freedom.

Hayek leaves no doubt about the content of the order the law is supposed to defend and support: an order providing for the maximum of freedom that is possible in a society. Only a liberal order is the *cosmos* he wants, the Great Society; he traces the latter concept to Adam Smith.[38] He believes in the "one great tradition extending from the ancient Greeks and Cicero through the Middle Ages to the classical liberals like John Locke, David Hume, Immanuel Kant and the Scottish moral philosophers, down to various American statesmen of the nineteenth and twentieth centuries, for whom law and liberty could not exist apart from each other," ending up with a statement attributed to Karl Binding, "The Law (*Recht*) is an order of human liberty."[39] Law is an order of human freedom because it orders freedom, a vague meta-legal concept, by transmuting its parts into concrete liberties or rights. By means of this transmutation, the law economizes intangible freedom into tangible "properties," something the economist Hayek could not overlook.[40] For him, law is "the basis of freedom."[41] All these considerations make it clear that Hayek (who, significantly, discusses the purpose of the law in a chapter entitled "Nomos: The Law of Liberty"[42]), considers liberty the purpose of the law, and law a means for the achievement of freedom as the end.

Much as the law is a means, it is an important means for the protection of liberty. For Hayek, it is the most important

---

[36]*Ibid.*, pp. 113-114.

[37]Compare *The Constitution of Liberty*, pp. 20-21.

[38]*Rules and Order*, pp. 2, 14. To Hayek, the concept of "the Great Society," or, in Karl Popper's words, "the Open Society," "has probably not lost its suitability by its use as a political slogan by a recent American administration" (of President Lyndon Johnson). *Rules and Order*, p. 148 n. 11.

[39]*Rules and Order*, pp. 52, 158 n. 15.

[40]Compare the author's *Über Formulierung der Menschenrechte* (Berlin, 1956); Hayek, *Rules and Order*, p. 121.

[41]*The Constitution of Liberty*, p. 148. See also p. 161.

[42]*Rules and Order*, pp. 94-123.

means, liberty's *conditio sine qua non.* This is evident in his comments on the rule of law. In *The Road to Serfdom*, he writes: "Nothing distinguishes more clearly conditions in a free country from those in a country under arbitrary government than the observance in the former of the great principles known as the Rule of Law." Two pages later, he refers to "the great liberal principle of the Rule of Law." "The Rule of Law was consciously evolved only during the liberal age and is one of its greatest achievements, not only as a safeguard but as the legal embodiment of freedom."[43] About a decade later, Hayek praises the rule of law "which for three hundred years has been the Englishman's ideal of freedom and which has become the example for the continental concept of the Rechtsstaat ... one of the ... achievements of Western culture." Quoting Radbruch, he writes: "Though democracy is certainly a praiseworthy value, the *Rechtsstaat* is like the daily bread, the water we drink and the air we breathe; and the greatest merit of democracy is that it alone is adapted to preserve the *Rechtsstaat.*"[44] The latter quotation is repeated in *The Constitution of Liberty*, where Hayek considers the rule of law "the basic conception of the law of liberty" and, quoting Holdsworth, states that it "is as valuable a principle today as it has ever been," and even goes so far as to claim that the rule of law is "more than constitutionalism."[45]

Hayek's respect for the rule of law, expressed in so many words, also can be concluded from the central position he assigns its discussion in *The Road to Serfdom* and *The Constitution of Liberty*. Looking at that position, the reader is reminded of the central location of clause 39 of the Magna Carta, the clause Hayek considers "the most famous and later most influential clause of Magna Carta,"[46] which states that "no free man shall be taken, imprisoned, outlawed, banished, or in any way destroyed ... except by the lawful judgment of his peers and by the law of the land." In the foreword to

---

[43] *The Road to Serfdom*, pp. 54, 56, 61.
[44] "Entstehung und Verfall des Rechtsstaatsideales," pp. 33, 57, 61.
[45] *The Constitution of Liberty*, pp. 248, 148, 489 n. 23, 205.
[46] *Ibid.*, p. 457 n. 4.

the 1956 American paperback edition of *The Road to Serfdom* Hayek expresses his "hope to supplement the all-too-brief central chapter of this book by a more extensive treatment of the relation between equality and justice."[47] The chapter he has in mind is the one on the rule of law, entitled "Planning and the Rule of Law." He sketched its supplement in *The Political Ideal of the Rule of Law* (Cairo, 1955), and elaborated it in *The Constitution of Liberty*. In the latter work, consisting of three parts, the discussion of the rule of law takes up the central second part. In *Law, Legislation and Liberty*, finally, the idea of the rule of law is not merely discussed in the central part. It is the subject of the whole work.

For Hayek, then, the rule of law is inseparable from freedom. In a way he considers the rule of law the other side of freedom. Certainly, it is the prerequisite for the rights of the individual, or tangible liberties. The rule of law can be compared to a tree which, from the invisible strong roots of freedom, lets the fruits of liberty branch out and grow and shine in splendor. This whets our appetite to know more about it, and to get an idea of what Hayek had to say about the rule of law, aside from what already has been discussed. A more detailed discussion of the rule of law is imperative, especially in view of the fact that Hayek complains that the "expression 'liberty under the law' ... has become almost meaningless because both 'liberty' and 'law' no longer have a clear meaning."[48]

---

[47] "*The Road to Serfdom* after Twelve Years," reprinted in *Studies in Philosophy, Politics and Economics* (Chicago, 1967), p. 223. At the conference founding the Mont Pelerin Society in 1947, Hayek stated that the rule of law is "central to our problem" in his "Opening Address to a Conference at Mont Pèlerin," *Studies in Philosophy, Politics and Economics*, p. 156. The importance of the rule of law can also be gathered from the fact that at the end of *The Road to Serfdom*, he favors an international rule of law, as he does in "A Self-Generating Order for Society," in John Nef, ed., *Towards World Community* (The Hague, 1968), pp. 39-42. In the index to *The Constitution of Liberty*, "Rule of Law" has 39 subtitles, "Laws," 81; "Freedom," 81; and "Government," 71. Other topics have fewer subtitles.

[48] *Rules and Order*, p. 62. See also his statement in "A Self-Generating Order for Society," p. 42, that "few people have yet learnt what the rule of law means—and they are rapidly forgetting it."

The rule of law can indeed mean a great many things. Its meaning can be vague and indefinite or clear and definite. Montesquieu's statement on the many meanings of freedom could well be applied to the rule of law. For instance, law can mean the law of God as well as the law of nature, both of which have meant different things to different people. It can mean international as well as national law. We are here mainly concerned with the latter; that is, with rules that are enforceable in a given society, nation, or state.

Having decided on the kind of law we are going to discuss, the question is what the rule of law means. Hayek, who thinks that the classical exposition of that concept was given by A. V. Dicey,[49] traces its meaning back to earlier authors. He points out that Titus Livius wrote of "imperia legum potentiora quam hominum," a phrase referred to by Algernon Sidney and John Adams, and in Holland's translation of Livy of 1600 rendered as "the authority and *rule of laws*, more powerful and mighty than those of men."[50] Hayek writes that Harrington spoke of "the empire of laws, not of men," and that the bill of rights of the constitution of Massachusetts of 1780 favored "a government of laws, not of men."[51] For Hayek the rule of law is the opposite of the rule of men. He believes in the former.

This is, of course, an idealized concept for, strictly speaking, a rule of law not of men is a contradiction in terms. It is obvious that in a society that is composed of men and in which law is accepted, made, and enforced by men, only men can let the law rule. The rule of law may be the best or worst rule by the best or worst men according to the best or worst laws made by the best or worst men. (*La loi, c'est moi.*) Clearly, this kind of rule would be a rule of men. However, since it is a rule according to the (best or worst) laws, it would also be a rule of law. On the other hand, it certainly would not qualify as a rule of law in the sense of the ideal "rule of law, not men." What is that rule of law like in reality?

---

[49] *The Road to Serfdom*, p. 54 n. 5.
[50] *The Constitution of Liberty*, p. 462 n. 33.
[51] *Ibid.*, pp. 166, 182.

It can be two things, depending on what we understand under law. If we think of law in the sense of *diritto, droit,* or *Recht,* law means what Sir Edward Coke had in mind when he thought of the "artificial reason of the law"—a body of right law accumulated over the ages with the help of great legal minds, a law that controls the ruler.[52] Law here rules the ruler as well as his subjects. Law precedes, and has priority over, the state, as is well symbolized by the German *Rechtsstaat.* If, on the other hand, we think of law in the sense of *legge, loi,* or *Gesetz,* law means what Coke called the "natural reason of the law," the kind of law desired by James I—a body of law desired by the ruler and accumulated during his rule or the rule of whoever might hold power. The ruler here makes the law for his subjects, and whether the law shall also be binding upon himself depends upon his pleasure. Law thus emanates from and comes after the state, as is well symbolized by the German *Staatsrecht.*[53] The Law State and State Law, then, are the two concepts of the rule of law.[54]

They are not necessarily opposites. Just as *legge* may be quite compatible with *diritto, loi* with *droit,* and *Gesetz* with *Recht,* and their enforcement may actually be a necessity for justice, so the law of the state may be quite compatible with the just state, and its enforcement be a prerequisite for that state.[55] This is recognized by Hayek.[56]

On the other hand, the rule of law in the sense of *Rechtsstaat* or Law State or the just state may well be jeopardized by the rule of law in the sense of *Staatsrecht* or State Law. Hayek's ideas on the latter possibility will be shown in the following pages.

---

[52] On Coke's discussion with James I, see Carl J. Friedrich, *Constitutional Government and Democracy* (Rev. ed., Boston, 1950), p. 103.

[53] I am using the term "Staatsrecht" not in its narrow, technical sense as it is used by German jurists, meaning a part of public law, but in a broader sense, meaning all law that can be enforced in any given state by those who govern.

[54] An elaboration of these concepts can be found in the author's *Two Concepts of the Rule of Law* (Indianapolis, 1973).

[55] *Ibid.,* pp. 13-15, 53-97.

[56] See pp. 133-145.

*Freedom through the Law State*

To Hayek, the rule of law is an ideal that was elaborated and realized most during the liberal era.

The quality of the rule of law as an ideal is already evident in *The Road to Serfdom*.[57] In 1953, he published an article on the emergence and decline of the ideal of the *Rechtsstaat*.[58] Two years later, his lectures in commemoration of the fiftieth anniversary of the National Bank of Egypt were printed under the title *The Political Ideal of the Rule of Law*.[59] In *The Constitution of Liberty*, a work planned to develop the argument of these lectures "on a larger canvass," he leaves no doubt that he considers the rule of law an ideal.[60] That ideal hovers over *Rules and Order*, the first volume of *Law, Legislation and Liberty*, all of which is concerned with the realization and negation of the rule of law.

In a large measure, Hayek uses the term "rule of law" in the sense of *Rechtsstaat*. As a matter of fact, he considers the *Rechtsstaat* the German version of the rule of law as it developed in England until the end of the eighteenth century, although it was more comprehensive and systematic than English law as a result of the stronger establishment on the continent of absolute monarchy.[61] Small wonder that to him the rule of law is prior to the state, in tune with the priority of "*Recht*" to "*Staat*" in the word "*Rechtsstaat*." Meta-legal freedom, from which the various rights of man derive, is thus matched by the meta-legal rule of law, serving as a guideline for human lawmaking. In *The Political Ideal of the Rule of Law*, we read: "The Rule of Law, as a limitation on the power of all government, is, of course, also a rule, but, as we

---

[57] *The Road to Serfdom*, p. 61.
[58] "Entstehung und Verfall des Rechtsstaatsideales," esp. pp. 33, 35.
[59] *The Political Ideal of the Rule of Law* (Cairo, 1955), p. 2.
[60] *The Constitution of Liberty*, pp. 164-166, 171. See also *The Political Ideal of the Rule of Law*, Preface.
[61] *The Road to Serfdom*, p. 58; "Entstehung and Verfall des Rechtsstaatsideales," p. 246; *The Political Ideal of the Rule of Law*, pp. 18-29; *The Constitution of Liberty*, pp. 196-204.

shall see, an extra-legal rule which cannot itself be a law but can only exist as the governing opinion about the attributes good laws should possess." It is a "Meta-Legal Principle . . . not a rule of the law but a rule about the law, a meta-legal doctrine, or a political ideal."[62] In *The Constitution of Liberty*, Hayek writes that the rule of law "is a doctrine concerning what the law ought to be, concerning the general attributes that particular laws should possess . . . not a rule of the law, but a rule concerning what the law ought to be, a meta-legal doctrine or a political ideal. It will be effective only in so far as the legislator feels bound by it."[63] This normative character of the rule of law is also evident in *Law, Legislation and Liberty*, a work that is mainly concerned with the obligations the rule of law, or *"the law* in the proper meaning of the word,"[64] upon the men who make laws at any particular time for any particular purpose. And the obligations prescribed by the rule of law, the ought of *the law*, have a major purpose, namely, the prevention of arbitrariness for the sake of the freedom of the individual.

In view of this imperative of the rule of law, the legal order corresponding to the ideal of the rule of law develops in liberty. It is a spontaneous order. It is not planned, as, for instance, by legislation. It gradually evolves by custom and the (largely judicial) finding of the law.[65] In his Cairo lectures Hayek mentioned the idea of a spontaneous order when he discussed law and order in connection with the safeguards of individual liberty. "Where intelligent human beings form the elements of such an order," he writes, "men

---

[62] *The Political Ideal of the Rule of Law*, pp. 25-26, 32-33. See also "Entstehung und Verfall des Rechtsstaatsideales," p. 45.

[63] *The Constitution of Liberty*, pp. 205-206.

[64] *Rules and Order*, p. 85. There does not seem to be much of a difference for Hayek between the rule of law and what he refers to in *Rules and Order* as "the law." As a matter of fact, on p. 85 he speaks of *"the law* in the proper meaning of the word, as contained in such expressions as the 'rule' or 'reign of law,' a 'government under the law'." On the other hand, it seems as if "the law" is something more concrete than a mere ideal, a transmutation, if only a partial one, of the ideal into law discovered and accepted by men. Compare p. 124.

[65] This does not mean, however, that Hayek would find legislation altogether incompatible with the rule of law or the spontaneous order. For him, "grown law requires correction by legislation." *Rules and Order*, p. 88.

whom we wish to use their individual knowledge as successfully as possible in the pursuit of their individual ends, we
must desire to bring about a mutual adjustment of the individual plans and actions by each adapting himself to those
circumstances which he can himself observe. The two devices
for this purpose on which man has tumbled and on which our
civilization has been built are that every man has a known
sphere of things which we can control and which we call his
property, and that these things can be transferred from the
sphere of one to that of another only by mutual consent.
These two general principles are of course capable of a great
deal of variety in detail—indeed the different systems of
private law are little more than variations on this theme."[66]
He confirms the idea of a spontaneous order in *The Constitution of Liberty*, favoring this kind of an "Order without
Commands," which "is what M. Polanyi has called the spontaneous formation of a 'polycentric order.' "[67]

Later, he repeatedly elaborates on that order. In 1963 he
devotes an essay to it.[68] Three years later, at the meeting of
the Mont Pelerin Society in Tokyo, he submitted a paper on
"The Principles of a Liberal Social Order," praising that order.
Adopting a term of Oakeshott, Hayek writes that "we may
call such a free society a *nomocratic* (law-governed) as distinguished from an unfree *telocratic* (purpose-governed) social
order."[69] In a 1967 article, "The Results of Human Action
but not of Human Design," he describes the spontaneous legal

---

[66] *The Political Ideal of the Rule of Law*, pp. 31-32.

[67] *The Constitution of Liberty*, p. 160. He quotes Polanyi: "When order is
achieved among human beings by allowing them to interact with each other on
their own initiative—subject only to the laws which uniformly apply to all of
them—we have a system of spontaneous order in society. We may then say that
the efforts of these individuals are co-ordinated by exercising their individual
initiative and that this self-co-ordination justifies this liberty on public
grounds.—The actions of such individuals are said to be free, for they are not
determined by any *specific* command, whether of a superior or a public authority;
the compulsion to which they are subject is impersonal and general."

[68] "Arten der Ordnung." This idea is also expressed during that year in the
essay "The Legal and Political Philosophy of David Hume," pp. 113-114.

[69] "The Principles of a Liberal Social Order," in *Essays in Philosophy, Politics
and Economics*, pp. 162-166 especially. The reference to Oakeshott is on page
163.

order created through the law. "Law is not only much older than legislation or even an organized state: the whole authority of the legislator and of the state derives from pre-existing conceptions of justice, and no system of articulated law can be applied except within a framework of generally recognized but often unarticulated rules of justice."[70] During the same year Hayek delivered his "Rechtsordnung und Handelnsordnung" at the University of Freiburg, a study on legal order and the order of acting. This work was his most elaborate and detailed treatise on the spontaneous legal order since he first touched on that subject; about half of the printed space is taken up by footnotes, an indication of how great a concern was the idea of spontaneous order.[71] This concern is evident in "A Self-Generating Order for Society," published in 1969. It can be seen in his latest work, *Law, Legislation and Liberty*, the first volume of which (*Rules and Order*) deals entirely with this spontaneous order. In *The Constitution of Liberty* Hayek "attempted to restate . . . the traditional doctrine of liberal constitutionalism." In his own words, what led him to write *Law, Legislation and Liberty*, "another book on the same general theme as the earlier one was the recognition that the preservation of a society of free men depends on three fundamental insights which have never been adequately expounded and to which the three main parts of this book are devoted. The first of these is that a self-generating or spontaneous order and an organization are distinct, and that their distinctiveness is related to the two different kinds of rules or laws which prevail in them. The second is that what today is generally regarded as 'social' or distributive justice has meaning only within the second of these kinds of order, the organization; but that it is meaningless in, and wholly incompatible with, that spontaneous order which Adam Smith called 'the Great Society', and Sir Karl Popper called 'the Open Society'. The third is that the predominant model of

---

[70]"The Results of Human Action but not of Human Design," in *Essays in Philosophy, Politics and Economics*, p. 102.

[71]"Rechtsordnung und Handelnsordnung," in *Freiburger Studien* (Tübingen, 1969), pp. 161-198.

liberal democratic institutions, in which the same representative body lays down the rules of just conduct and directs
government, necessarily leads to a gradual transformation of
the spontaneous order of a free society into a totalitarian
system conducted in the service of some coalition of organized interests."[72] According to these words in the introduction to *Rules and Order*, we may expect all three volumes
of *Law, Legislation and Liberty* to defend the spontaneous
order.

In that order, all men in society—subjects as well as
rulers—are bound by the rule of law, which through a slow
evolutionary process becomes condensed into what Hayek in
*Rules and Order* refers to as "*the* law," "lawyer's law," "the
law," and "*the law*."[73] It corresponds to "the *nomos* of the
ancient Greeks and the *ius* of the Romans (and what in other
European languages is distinguished as *droit, Recht,* or *diritto*
from the *loi, Gesetz,* or *legge*)."[74] It is the body of law that
to Hayek is just because it corresponds to the ideal of the
rule of law. If not identical to that ideal, *the law* is at least a
partial realization of the ideal. Having been spontaneously—
and thus freely—discovered throughout the ages, and having
been accepted for generations in a more or less natural way
and thus considered natural, it is some kind of a realization of
justice, perhaps the moral idea, and thus assumes a role
similar to that of the state in the philosophy of Hegel. And
just as for the German idealist the state as the realization of
the moral idea is the march of God in the world, for the consti-
tutionalist, the "Old Whig" Hayek, that march is the (rule of)
law as the realization of the liberal idea of justice. Under it,
there exists "The State of Liberty."[75]

The editor of *Capitalism and the Historians* (1954) takes an
historical approach when he shows the gradual and slow
growth of the concept of the rule of law and the spontaneously and freely accepted *law*. "Law in the sense of
enforced rules of conduct is undoubtedly coeval with society;

---

[72] *Rules and Order*, p. 2.
[73] *Ibid.*, pp. 67, 82, 85, 94, 124, 126, 127, 128, 134.
[74] *Ibid.*, p. 94.
[75] *The Political Ideal of the Rule of Law*, p. 4.

only the observance of common rules makes the peaceful existence of individuals in society possible. Long before man had developed language to the point where it enabled him to issue general commands, an individual would be accepted as a member of a group only so long as he conformed to its rules."[76] The rule of law can be seen in the Greek *isonomia*.[77] It was evident in ancient Rome.[78] It existed in the Middle Ages.[79] It can clearly be noted throughout English constitutional development.[80] Its acceptance, and the law made in conformity with it, up to the liberal era was more or less subconscious and natural, and in that era had become taken for granted.[81] The ideal was firmly established in England during the seventeenth and eighteenth centuries, and England taught the ideal of the rule of law to the world.[82] It

[76] *Rules and Order*, pp. 72-73. Previously in "Arten der Ordnung," p. 10.

[77] "Entstehung und Verfall des Rechtsstaatsideales," pp. 33-37; *The Political Ideal of the Rule of Law*, pp. 6-8; *The Constitution of Liberty*, pp. 164-166; *Rules and Order*, pp. 52, 85.

[78] *The Road to Serfdom*, p. 61; "Entstehung und Verfall des Rechtsstaatsideales," pp. 37-38; *The Political Ideal of the Rule of Law*, pp. 8-9; *The Constitution of Liberty*, pp. 166-167; *Rules and Order*, pp. 52, 82-83.

[79] *The Constitution of Liberty*, pp. 162-163; *Rules and Order*, pp. 52, 83. Hayek feels he can do no better than quote the main conclusions of Fritz Kern, *Kingship and Law in the Middle Ages* (London, 1939), p. 151: "When a case arises for which no valid law can be adduced, then the lawful men or doomsmen will make new law in the belief that what they are making is good old law, not indeed expressly handed-down, but tacitly existent. They do not, therefore, create the law: they 'discover' it. Any particular judgment in court, which we regard as a particular inference from a general established legal rule, was to the medieval mind in no way distinguishable from the legislative activity of the community; in both cases a law hidden but already existing is discovered, not created. There is, in the Middle Ages, no such thing as the 'first application of a legal rule'. Law is old; new law is a contradiction in terms; for either new law is derived explicitly or implicitly from the old, or it conflicts with the old, in which case it is not lawful. The fundamental idea remains the same; the old law is the true law, and the true law is the old law. According to medieval ideas, therefore, the enactment of new law is not possible at all; and all legislation and legal reform is conceived of as the restoration of the good old law which has been violated."

[80] *The Political Ideal of the Rule of Law*, p. 6; *Rules and Order*, p. 84.

[81] *The Road to Serfdom*, pp. 54, 61; "Entstehung und Verfall des Rechtsstaatsideales," p. 45; *The Political Ideal of the Rule of Law*, p. 13; *The Constitution of Liberty*, p. 173; *Rules and Order*, pp. 67-68, 73, "Rechtsordnung und Handelnsordnung," p. 182.

[82] "Entstehung und Verfall des Rechtsstaatsideales," pp. 33, 37-44; *The Political Ideal of the Rule of Law*, pp. 2, 9-13; *The Constitution of Liberty*, pp. 167-175; *Rules and Order*, pp. 52, 84-85.

was to be reflected in constitutional governments in the old and new worlds.[83]

Hayek explains what the ideal law is like. It must provide for a maximum of freedom in society. This is possible only if it meets certain prerequisites. Law must be general and "abstract"; addressed to all, as distinguished from special commands to specific persons. This idea was desired by the Petition of Grievances of 1610, the year of Dr. Bonham's Case. It is emphasized in the discussion concerning the Statute of Monopolies of 1624, in Coke's interpretation of Magna Carta (1628), Locke's Second Treatise on Civil Government (1690), Hume's comments on the abolition of the Star Chamber (1762), in the writings of Sir Philip Francis and William Paley, of Montesquieu, Rousseau, and Condorcet. It is an important feature of the *Rechtsstaat*. Hayek approves of the definition of law in the Girondist draft for a constitution: "Les caractères qui distinguent les lois sont leur généralité et leur durée infinie."[84] General law implies the absence of privilege.[85] Hayek does not deny "that even general, abstract rules, equally applicable to all, may possibly constitute severe restrictions on liberty." However, he immediately adds: "But when we reflect on it, we see how very unlikely this is. The chief

---

[83]"Entstehung und Verfall des Rechtsstaatsideales," pp. 33, 45-56; *The Political Ideal of the Rule of Law*, pp. 2, 5, 13-23; *The Constitution of Liberty*, pp. 176-204; *Rules and Order*, p. 52. (The references in notes 76 to 83 generally refer to Hayek's references to the rule of law, with exception to the references to *Rules and Order*, which refer to "law." This gives the impression that for Hayek there is no real difference between the "rule of law" and the "law." In *Rules and Order*, pp. 82, 85, he mentions both expressions together, one obviously being identical to the other).

[84]*The Road to Serfdom*, pp. 54, 56; "Entstehung und Verfall des Rechtsstaatsideales," pp. 39-56; *The Political Ideal of the Rule of Law*, pp. 34-35; *The Constitution of Liberty*, pp. 148-161, 188; "Ursachen der ständigen Gefährdung der Freiheit," p. 106; "Arten der Ordnung," pp. 4, 11, 15, 17-20; "Legal and Political Philosophy of David Hume," pp. 114-116; "Principles of a Liberal Social Order," pp. 162, 168; "Die Verfassung eines freien Staates," in Franz Böhm, Friedrich A. Lutz, Fritz W. Meyer, eds., *Ordo* XIX (1968), p. 4; "A Self-Generating Order for Society," p. 40; *Rules and Order*, pp. 48, 50-51, 138, 169, 176-178, 180-181, 185, 192-195.

[85]*The Political Ideal of the Rule of Law*, pp. 9-11; *The Constitution of Liberty*, pp. 153-154, 167-170; earlier already in *The Road to Serfdom*, p. 59; "Entstehung und Verfall des Rechtsstaatsideales," pp. 38-56.

safeguard is that the rules must apply to those who lay them down and those who apply them—that is, to the government as well as the governed—and that nobody has the power to grant exceptions. If all that is prohibited and enjoined is prohibited and enjoined for all without exception (unless such exception follows from another general rule) and if even authority has no special powers except that of enforcing the law, little that anybody may reasonably wish to do is likely to be prohibited."[86] In Hayek's view equal, abstract rules for all are conducive to freedom.

For the sake of freedom, equal laws for all must be complemented by the equality of all before the law. Hayek connected these two features in 1955, when he wrote that "the requirement of generality touches most closely on the second, most difficult and perhaps most important requirement, that of *equality* before the law."[87] In *The Constitution of Liberty*, he elaborates that equality before the law, connecting it with the idea that it is conducive to liberty: "The great aim of the struggle for liberty has been equality before the law. This equality under the rules which the state enforces may be supplemented by a similar equality of the rules that men voluntarily obey in their relations with one another. This extension of the principle of equality to the rules of moral and social conduct is the chief expression of what is commonly called the democratic spirit—and probably that aspect of it that does most to make inoffensive the inequalities that liberty necessarily produces." He continues: "Equality of the general rules of law and conduct, however, is the only kind of equality conducive to liberty and the only equality which we can secure without destroying liberty."[88] Generally speaking, equality competes with freedom. The equality of all before a law being conducive to freedom, however, is quite in order; it is a liberal's concession to democracy, a characteristic feature of liberal democracy.

Another quality of the law securing liberty is certainty,

---

[86] *The Constitution of Liberty*, pp. 154-155.

[87] *The Political Ideal of the Rule of Law*, p. 35. See also *The Road to Serfdom*, p. 59; "Entstehung und Verfall des Rechtsstaatsideales," p. 57.

[88] *The Constitution of Liberty*, p. 85.

"which for the functioning of the economic activities of society is probably the most important." Hayek doubts "whether the significance which the certainty of the law has for the smooth and efficient working of economic life can be exaggerated, and there is probably no single factor which has contributed more to the greater prosperity of the Western World compared with the Orient than the relative certainty of the law which in the West had early been achieved."[89] In *The Constitution of Liberty*, Hayek in a way repeats this statement, now calling certainty the "second chief attribute which must be required of true laws" and equality before the law the "third requirement of true law," with generality retaining its original first position.[90]

For a further protection of liberty, Hayek cites additional elements of that "complex of principles which secure a reign of law."[91] These institutional devices, designed to weaken the power of the state and thus to strengthen the freedom of the individuals are: separation of powers—division of the government into executive, legislative, and judicial branches—so that one branch, for the sake of liberty, might check the other;[92] federalism as a means for the protection of the individual from big, centralized government;[93] bills of rights that guarantee men a free sphere upon which the public power is not permitted to intrude;[94] limitations upon administrative discretion[95] and upon legislative discretion;[96] written consti-

---

[89] *The Political Ideal of the Rule of Law*, p. 36.

[90] *The Constitution of Liberty*, pp. 208-209. This is a slight shift from the position taken in *The Political Ideal of the Rule of Law*, as far as the ranking of equality and certainty is concerned.

[91] *The Political Ideal of the Rule of Law*, p. 13. See also "Entstehung und Verfall des Rechtsstaatsideales," p. 44; *The Constitution of Liberty*, p. 218.

[92] "Entstehung und Verfall des Rechtsstaatsideales," pp. 46-47; *The Political Ideal of the Rule of Law*, pp. 16, 37-39; *The Constitution of Liberty*, pp. 169-170, 178, 183-184, 210-212; *Rules and Order*, pp. 128-131.

[93] *The Constitution of Liberty*, pp. 183-186.

[94] *The Political Ideal of the Rule of Law*, pp. 13-15, 43-45; *The Constitution of Liberty*, pp. 182-183.

[95] "Entstehung und Verfall des Rechtsstaatsideales," pp. 50-56; *The Political Ideal of the Rule of Law*, pp. 15, 19-25, 39-42; *The Constitution of Liberty*, pp. 193-204, 212-214; *Rules and Order*, esp. pp. 137-140.

[96] "Entstehung und Verfall des Rechtsstaatsideales," p. 45; *The Political Ideal of the Rule of Law*, pp. 42-43; *The Constitution of Liberty*, pp. 178-179, 186-192, 214-217; *Rules and Order*, esp. pp. 128-131.

tutions that are compatible with the rule of law;[97] and judicial review as a means of securing limited government and the rights of men.[98] In accordance with all this, Hayek feels that in a liberal society, the bulk of the law should be private and that public law should be reduced to a minimum.[99]

His strong defense of freedom through the rule of law and its spirit, his protection of liberal law through institutional devices, make Hayek comparable to the author of *The Spirit of the Laws*, one of the great liberals of all times—Montesquieu.[100]

In the modern era, an era characterized by the march of democracy, the rule of law has declined, in Hayek's opinion. This decline and the ensuing road to serfdom is the sad fact, the big fear evident in his writing in social philosophy. "One could write a history of the decline of the Rule of Law, the disappearance of the *Rechtsstaat*," he wrote in 1944,[101] and in the following years he did so. In 1953 he published his article on the emergence and decline of the *Rechtsstaat*, an article that ends with a disturbing account of "the destruction of the Rechtsstaat." His last lecture in Cairo was entitled "The Decline of the Rule of Law." In *The Constitution of Liberty* he devoted a chapter to "The Decline of the Law." *Rules and Order*, the first volume of *Law, Legislation and Liberty*, is concerned with threats to the rule of law and to freedom.

The title of that work indicates the essence of that decline: the increasing replacement of traditional law through legislation at the cost of liberty. A quotation of Lord Acton at the head of the chapter on the decline of the law in *The Con-*

---

[97] *The Political Ideal of the Rule of Law*, p. 14; *The Constitution of Liberty*, pp. 169, 178-182.

[98] *The Constitution of Liberty*, pp. 186-192.

[99] *Ibid.*, pp. 220-233, 234-249; "Principles of a Liberal Social Order," pp. 168-169; *Rules and Order*, pp. 141-143.

[100] In *Rules and Order*, p. 4, Hayek writes, concerning the plan for *Law, Legislation and Liberty*: "I soon discovered that to carry out what I had undertaken would require little less than doing for the twentieth century what Montesquieu had done for the eighteenth. The reader will believe me when I say that in the course of the work I more than once despaired of my ability to come even near the aim I had set myself."

[101] *The Road to Serfdom*, p. 58.

*stitution of Liberty* hints at the seriousness of that decline:
"The dogma, that absolute power may, by the hypothesis of
popular origin, be as legitimate as constitutional freedom,
began ... to darken the air." So does a quotation from
William Pitt at the head of the Cairo lecture: "Necessity is the
plea for every infringement of human freedom. It is the
argument of tyrants; it is the creed of slaves." According to
the democratic dogma of necessity, whatever governmental
power executing popular desires may consider necessary at
any particular moment and enact into laws is as legitimate as
traditional law even though it is detrimental to freedom.
Under the principle *lex posterior derogat priori* legislation
even supersedes traditional law. At the expense of freedom,
law has moved a long way from the general acceptance of the
Bractonian principle, *non sub homine sed sub Deo et lege*, in
the liberal era to the slogan, *vox populi vox dei*, from the
French Revolution forward.

Hayek is not opposed to democracy as such; he sees in it
an important means for the protection of freedom.[102]
Agreeing with Meinecke and Hume that the sense of English
history has been the development from a government of men
to one of law,[103] he knows that the growth of popular
government up to the nineteenth century had a fair share in
this development. Hayek also does not resent the democratic
French Revolution as such. After all, friends of the rule of
law, such as Montesquieu, Rousseau, and Condorcet, had
contributed to that revolution. "There is a great deal of truth
in it, at least in so far as the beginning of the Revolution and
the aims of the more moderate groups are concerned, when
the historian Michelet describes it in a memorable phrase as
*l'avènement de la loi*. Much of its work was guided by the
ideal of a government of law."[104] However, an *avènement de
la loi* is not necessarily an *avènement du droit*.[105] The trend
toward legislation, enormously boosted by the French Revolu-

---

[102]*The Constitution of Liberty*, pp. 103-117.
[103]"Entstehung und Verfall des Rechtsstaatsideales," p. 42; "Legal and Political Philosophy of David Hume," p. 110.
[104]*The Political Ideal of the Rule of Law*, p. 17.
[105]Compare pp. 118-119.

tion, resulted in a situation in which legislative acts, made on the spur of the moment for reasons of expediency and backed by the school of positivism, could well ignore the rule of law and infringe upon freedom.

Hayek laments this situation: "The substantive conception of the *Rechtsstaat*, which required that the rules of law possess definite properties, was displaced by a purely formal concept which required merely that all action of the state be authorized by the legislature. In short, a 'law' was that which merely stated that whatever a certain authority did should be legal. . . . By the turn of the century it had become accepted doctrine that the 'individualist' ideal of the substantive *Rechtsstaat* was a thing of the past, 'vanquished by the creative powers of national and social ideas.' " With deep concern, Hayek quotes Bernatzik's evaluation of the situation shortly before World War I: "We have returned to the principles of the police state [!] to such an extent that we again recognize the idea of a *Kulturstaat*. The only difference is in the means. On the basis of laws the modern state permits itself everything, much more than the police state did. Thus, in the course of the nineteenth century, the term *Rechtsstaat* was given a new meaning. We understand by it a state whose whole activity takes place on the basis of laws and in legal form. On the purpose of the state and the limits of its competence the term *Rechtsstaat* in its present-day meaning says nothing."[106]

The decline of law was aggravated after Hans Kelsen expounded his Pure Theory of Law in the 1920s. Kelsen stated that, as he put it, the fundamentally irretrievable liberty of the individual gradually recedes into the background and the liberty of the social collective occupies the front of the stage and that this change in the conception of freedom meant an emancipation of democratism from liberalism. Hayek notes that under the Pure Theory of Law, "the *Rechtsstaat* becomes an extremely formal concept and

---

[106] *The Constitution of Liberty*, pp. 237-238. See also "Entstehung und Verfall des Rechtsstaatsideales," pp. 57-59; *The Political Ideal of the Rule of Law*, pp. 49-52.

an attribute of all states, even a despotic one. There are no possible limits to the power of the legislator, and there are no 'so-called fundamental liberties'; and any attempt to deny to an arbitrary despotism the character of a legal order represents 'nothing but the naiveté and presumption of natural-law thinking.' " Hayek further denounces the Pure Theory of Law: "Every effort is made not only to obscure the fundamental distinction between true laws in the substantive sense of abstract, general rules and laws in the merely formal sense (including all acts of the legislature) but also to render indistinguishable from them the orders of any authority, no matter what they are, by including them all in the vague term 'norm.' "[107]

Thus, although scholars including Hayek contrasted the liberal *Rechtsstaat* with the communist, fascist, socialist, and national-socialist state,[108] it could be asserted, under the doctrine of legal positivism, the Pure Theory of Law, and the "normative-order-thinking" of Carl Schmitt,[109] that every state, no matter how despotic, was in tune with the rule of law; that even the Third Reich was a *Rechtsstaat*.[110] Therefore, not only was the decline of the rule of law the road to serfdom, serfdom also found its basis in the law by which despots ruled. The traditional emphasis upon private law was replaced by one on public law. Law regulating individuals from above became more important than law grown among them in freedom.

Serfdom is probably the most obvious under the tyranny of one ruler, and perhaps the most oppressive if that ruler is backed by the majority. This may well be the reason why modern totalitarianism is more dangerous to liberty than the absolutism prior to the liberal era. Much as Hayek was aware of the despotism of Hitler, he was aware that it was a popular despotism. He also clearly recognized that the road to this

---

[107] *The Constitution of Liberty*, p. 238. In this quotation and others, numbers referring to sources are omitted.

[108] *Ibid.*, p. 239.

[109] *Rules and Order*, p. 71.

[110] On those who considered the national socialist regime a *Rechtsstaat*, including Schmitt, see my *Two Concepts of the Rule of Law*, pp. 36-37.

kind of tyranny was the natural outcome of the replacement of the traditional rule of law and its liberal values by democratic legislation and administrative regulations on the basis of legislation. This is a plain message of *The Road to Serfdom*. It remains a thesis of his later work, which never loses sight of the danger of democratic despotism when, after the fall of fascism and national socialism, democracy more or less became the order of the day. Like many of his articles, Hayek's two larger studies in social thought since World War II clearly express this fact. *The Constitution of Liberty* suggests ways and means to secure freedom in a democratic society. The control of democratic legislation which in a large measure is social legislation providing for social organization and management, by the traditional rule of law providing for freedom, plays a major role in that book. *Law, Legislation and Liberty* seems to concentrate on that control. It emphasizes the "scientific error" through which legislation, cornered as it should be by law and liberty, has increasingly been encouraged to corner liberty and law. This to Hayek is "the great tragedy of our time—a tragedy, because the values which scientific error tends to dethrone are the indispensable foundation of our civilization."[111] Resuming his analyses where Hume and Kant had left off, Hayek, juxtaposing the law of liberty to that of legislation, demonstrates that the former rather than the latter is conducive to the great society in the sense of Adam Smith, a society that results from human action rather than from human design and is a freely grown, spontaneous rather than an imposed, planned society.

*The Necessity of State Law*[112]

Hayek's skepticism toward legislation must not conceal the fact that he attributes important functions to it.

Since legislation constitutes part of State Law or *Staatsrecht* as understood in a broad sense, Hayek, who as an "unrepentant Old Whig" never tires of emphasizing the danger

---

[111] *Rules and Order*, pp. 6-7.

[112] The following remarks were prepared as a paper for a conference on Hayek's legal philosophy, sponsored by The Institute of Humane Studies and the Liberty Fund, Inc., in San Francisco, January, 1976.

of State Law to the Law State, of *Staatsrecht* to the *Rechts-staat*, thus admits the importance of the former for the latter. Clearly distinguishing between *diritto, droit, Recht,* or (right) law, and *legge, loi, Gesetz,* or (not necessarily right) law, he goes out of his way to stress that the latter might not be identical to, and might be incompatible with, the former.[113] On the other hand, he also makes clear that the two may well be in harmony.

This is evident already in *The Road to Serfdom*: "The Rule of Law ... implies limits to the scope of legislation: it restricts it to the kind of general rules known as formal law and excludes legislation either directly aimed at particular people or at enabling anybody to use the coercive power of the state for the purpose of such discrimination. It means, not that everything is regulated by law, but, on the contrary, that the coercive power of the state can be used only in cases defined in advance by the law and in such a way that it can be foreseen how it will be used. A particular enactment can thus infringe the Rule of Law."[114] It must not do so. As long as legislation establishes general rules known as formal law and is not either directly aimed at particular people or at enabling anybody to use the coercive power of the state for the purpose of such discrimination, it is compatible with the rule of law.

In his Cairo lectures, Hayek again attributes an important place to legislation. Together with adjudication, it will tend to approach the ideal of the rule of law "more and more."[115] This is evident when he discusses the generality, equality, and certainty of the law, the separation of powers, administrative discretion, legislation and policy. He describes legislative acts "which decide about the use of the means which are put at the state's disposal" and "are in effect orders to its servants." He indicates regrets that such acts "are also called laws" because they are not generally valid for everybody. On the other hand, some legislative acts constitute general rules and are "true laws in the specific sense in which we distinguish

---

[113] *Rules and Order*, p. 94.

[114] *The Road to Serfdom*, pp. 83-84.

[115] *The Political Ideal of the Rule of Law*, p. 33.

laws from orders." This kind of legislation is in conformity with the rule of law and is conducive to the freedom of the individual.[116] The same applies to legislation that binds the administration: "It would certainly not be compatible with the Rule of Law if this was interpreted to mean that in its dealings with the private citizen the administration is not always subject to the law laid down by the legislature and applied by independent courts." The legislature may delegate powers to make rules for the protection of the individual from the administration to some other body. In that case, that body would act according to legislation which corresponds to the rule of law.[117] Finally, Hayek regrets that in current usage the distinction between legislation and policy is often obscured, writing that "there is good sense in it where the two concepts are deliberately contrasted." While he admits that in a certain sense legislation always involves policy, namely, long-run policy, he points to the danger of short-term policy which is to be contrasted with legislation.[118]

In *The Constitution of Liberty*, these remarks are repeated.[119] In a way that is reminiscent of Sir Edward Coke when he talked about the artificial reason of the law that has been built up over the ages by great jurists, Hayek writes that legislation has the important function of adding the contributions of speculative thinkers, after they have passed through a long process of selection and modification in the course of time, to the body of the law. He quotes at length Dicey's classical description of law making, according to which legislation reflects more than the desires of the day. It also reveals the opinions of yesterday, and can be considered an amendment of the laws as they have existed for ages. Legislation can be in the mainstream of the evolution of the rule of law, and make an important contribution to that rule.[120]

---

[116]*Ibid.*, p. 35.

[117]*Ibid.*, p. 38.

[118]*Ibid.*, pp. 42-43.

[119]*The Constitution of Liberty*, pp. 211, 214-215.

[120]*Ibid.*, p. 113. The quotation from A. V. Dicey reads: "The opinion which changes the law is in one sense the opinion of the time when the law is actually altered; in another sense it has often been in England the opinion prevalent some twenty or thirty years before that time; it has been as often as not in reality the

The title, *Law, Legislation and Liberty*, shows a fundamental distinction between law and legislation. The first volume, *Rules and Order*, devotes a chapter to "Nomos: The Law of Liberty," and one to "Thesis: The Law of Legislation." The former is good. The latter, bad, or at least dubious and quite possibly and probably at variance with the law of liberty. This is the gist of these chapters. Yet in spite of all emphasis upon the threat of legislation to the rule of law and freedom, Hayek, in a chapter on the changing concept of the law, shows why "grown law requires correction by legislation." He thus admits the value of legislation in a way that reminds us of the admission, centuries ago, of the value of equity as a corrective of the common law. He concedes that the "case for relying even in modern times for the development of law on the gradual process of judicial precedent and scholarly interpretation has been persuasively argued by the late Bruno Leoni, *Liberty and the Law* (Princeton, 1961)." Yet he does not agree with his friend Leoni, writing that "although his argument is an effective antidote to the prevailing orthodoxy which believes that only legislation can or ought to alter the law, it has not convinced me that we can dispense with legislation even in the field of private law with which it is chiefly concerned."[121]

Even the good law, arising out of the spontaneous endeavor to articulate rules of conduct, may "develop in very undesirable directions." And "when this happens correction by deliberate legislation may ... be the only practicable way out." The spontaneous growth of the law "may lead into an

---

opinion not of to-day but of yesterday. ... Legislative opinion must be the opinion of the day, because, when laws are altered, the alteration is of necessity carried into effect by legislators who act under the belief that the change is an amendment; but this law-making opinion is also the opinion of yesterday, because the beliefs which have at last gained such hold on the legislature as to produce an alteration in the law have generally been created by thinkers or writers, who exerted their influence long before the change in the law took place. Thus it may well happen that an innovation is carried through at a time when the teachers who supplied the arguments in its favour are in their graves, or even—and this is well worth noting—when in the world of speculation a movement has already set in against ideas which are exerting their full effect in the world of action and of legislation." p. 445 n. 15.

[121] *Rules and Order*, p. 168 n. 35.

impasse from which it cannot extricate itself by its own forces or which it will at least not correct quickly enough." He adds: "The development of case-law is in some respects a sort of one-way street: when it has already moved a considerable distance in one direction, it often cannot retrace its steps when some implications of earlier decisions are seen to be clearly undesirable. The fact that law that has evolved in this way has certain desirable properties does not prove that it will always be good law or even that some of its rules may not be very bad. It therefore does not mean that we can altogether dispense with legislation." Hayek even goes so far as to admit the necessity of "radical changes of particular rules" by legislation.[122] He thus seems to come close to the idea of a "motorized law-maker."[123]

The need for legislation follows from various considerations. One is the slow and gradual process of judicial development, which precludes a rapid adaptation of the law to wholly new circumstances, something Hayek considers desirable. The legislature must become active here, because the judges should use restraint in reversing "a development, which has already taken place and is then seen to have undesirable consequences or to be downright wrong . . . . The judge is not performing his function if he disappoints reasonable expectations created by earlier decisions." The judge ought to develop the law, not to alter it, at least not rapidly. Although the judge "may clearly recognize that another rule would be better, or more just, it would evidently be unjust to apply it to transactions which had taken place when a different rule was regarded as valid." Therefore, a new rule should be made known through legislation, fulfilling the proper function of all law, that of guiding expectations.

Hayek reveals himself as a liberal rather than a conservative when he stresses the liberating effect of legislation. More effectively than judicial decisions legislation may do away with injustices caused by the fact "that the development of the law has lain in the hands of members of a particular class

---

[122]*Ibid.*, pp. 88-89.
[123]Compare the author's *In Defense of Property* (Chicago, 1963), p. 152.

whose traditional views made them regard as just what could not meet the more general requirements of justice." In an obvious agreement with Marx, the honorary president of the Mont Pelerin Society writes that the law on the relations between master and servant, landlord and tenant, creditor and debtor, organized business and its customers, has been shaped in large measure by the views of the parties and their particular interests, especially in the first two instances, with masters and landlords almost exclusively supplying the judges. While he takes issue with Kelsen's assertion that "justice is an irrational ideal" and that "from the point of rational cognition there are only interests of human beings and hence conflicts of interests," Hayek admits that the interests of ruling groups may bring about law that, incompatible with justice and not measuring up to the ideal of the rule of law, should be replaced fast by legislation that corresponds to that ideal.[124]

The age of democracy is an age of legislation because legislation makes up the bulk of democratic law. It constitutes an important part of modern state law and, as Hayek pointed out again and again, a great threat to freedom and the rule of law.[125] However, as he has also shown, legislation can be an essential support of liberalism and the *Rechtsstaat*. Hayek praises legislation while he condemns it. This is not surprising. Although Hayek distinguishes *isonomia* or the rule of law and liberalism from democracy[126] and emphasizes that democratic development can be and has been a threat to the rule of law and to freedom, he also leaves no doubt that democratic development can be and has been an important part of the evolution of liberty and the rule of law. Stressing that "democracy is a means rather than an end," Hayek sees "three chief arguments by which democracy can be justified,

---

[124]*Rules and Order*, pp. 88-89.

[125]See pp. 121-122, 129-133.

[126]"Entstehung und Verfall des Rechtsstaatsideales," pp. 33-65; *The Political Ideal of the Rule of Law; The Constitution of Liberty*, esp. pp. 54-56, 103-104, 106, 162-219; "The Principles of a Liberal Social Order," p. 161; "Die Verfassung eines freien Staates," pp. 3-11.

each of which may be regarded as conclusive . . . . The first is that, whenever it is necessary that one of several conflicting opinions should prevail and when one would have to be made to prevail by force if need be, it is less wasteful to determine which has the stronger support by counting numbers than by fighting. Democracy is the only method of peaceful change that man has yet discovered." The second argument is that "democracy is an important safeguard of individual liberty," and that "the prospects of individual liberty are better in a democracy than under other forms of government." The third, and to Hayek the most powerful, argument is that the existence of democratic institutions will improve the general level of understanding public affairs. Agreeing with Tocqueville's "great work, *Democracy in America*," he writes "that democracy is the only effective method of educating the majority." The liberal who rejects conservatism because it is static, feels that democracy as a process of forming opinion must be given preference over a government by an elite which may be all too static, that the value of democracy proves itself in its dynamic aspects. At the end of his chief arguments in favor of democracy, Hayek ties up that form of government with liberty: "As is true of liberty, the benefits of democracy will show themselves only in the long run, while its more immediate achievements may well be inferior to those of other forms of government."[127]

To Hayek, then, democracy may well be conducive to freedom and the rule of law. In other words, the State Law (*Staatsrecht*) of liberal democracy, irrespective of whether it has grown slowly through custom or judicial decisions, or enacted by legislatures, can favor the Law State or *Rechtsstaat*, and its far-reaching realization of freedom.

Hayek goes further than maintaining that the law of the state can aid the rule of law. To him, *Staatsrecht* is a prerequisite for the *Rechtsstaat*.

One concept is a *sine qua non* for the other: its tangible, concrete aspect is necessary for the realization of the ideal or part of it. The rule of law does not merely imply a restriction

---

[127]*The Constitution of Liberty*, pp. 107-109.

of the government for the sake of the individual through the law. Law, as distinguished from ethics and morals, implies sanction by the government vis-a-vis individuals. So does "rule." Law being an ethical minimum,[128] it is the very essence of that minimum that it is enforceable. In view of the fact that all law in one way or another measures and restricts, law implies the absence of license. Although freedom is the predominant value in Hayek's social thought,[129] Hayek is not inclined toward anarchy. The latter word does not appear in the index to *The Road to Serfdom*, or in that to *The Constitution of Liberty*.[130] Hayek wants freedom under law. True freedom must be something tangible that cannot really exist without the protection of the laws. While the rule of the law of the state, just as the empire of men of which Harrington spoke,[131] can and does infringe upon the freedom of the individual, that freedom—that is, what remains of it in society—is protected by virtue of the law. It is the law that transforms parts of the general, vague, and intangible concept of freedom into specific and clearly defined tangible rights the individual can claim. As the title of his book shows, Hayek does not just believe in liberty. He believes in the *constitution* of liberty. He prefers a constituted liberty over a non-constituted one, even though the former may not be a transmutation into reality of freedom in its totality. Hayek favors a liberal constitution, a liberal order. To him, order is the prerequisite for freedom. While freedom is the great ideal that hovers over the legal order and always prompts that order to become more free, the legal order is the realization, if only partial, of the ideal. Hayek, perhaps in Hegelian measure, considers the real the rational.[132] The genuine liberal realizes that it is reasonable to accept the authority of the state, while always being wary of its power. *Potestas* is dangerous. *Auctoritas* is necessary.

[128]See Georg Jellinek, *Die sozialethische Bedeutung von Recht, Unrecht und Strafe* (2d ed., Berlin 1908), p. 45.

[129]See pp. 107-111.

[130]*Rules and Order* contains an index of names only.

[131]James Harrington, *The Common-wealth of Oceana* (London, 1656), p. 2.

[132]The liberalism of Hegel is brought out in Carl J. Friedrich's introduction to his edition of *The Philosophy of Hegel* (New York, 1954).

Different as they are, authority and power will usually co-exist. Even the most powerful government will possess some legitimate authority, just as even under the most liberal regimes there will be some aspects of power. The liberal aristocrat Friedrich August von Hayek expresses his kinship to liberals such as Burke[133] and de Tocqueville.[134] These men expressed serious misgivings about the French Revolution, an event that challenged royal absolutism and monarchical power. It is an interesting question whether Hayek resents revolution as a means for absolutely destroying an existing legal order for the sake of freedom. He shows his admiration for Schiller, author of *Die Räuber* and *Wilhelm Tell*, dramas in which legal orders based upon men's law are challenged by an appeal to the immutable rights of men that are, as it says in *Wilhelm Tell*, "hanging in heaven."[135] At the same time, Hayek often quotes Schiller's friend Goethe who, while he confessed that he could imagine to have committed every crime, observed when he saw innocent people hurt by the police in a riot, that it was better to have an injustice than to have disorder. Hayek mentions revolutions against regimes in which power and abuses of power were more obvious than authority, such as the revolutions against Charles I and Louis XVI.[136] Yet he does not seem to come out with a plain statement proposing a right of revolution, although he seems to be sympathetic to such revolutions.

This is obvious also from what he writes at the end of *The Constitution of Liberty*, in the chapter, "Why I am Not a Conservative," under the subtitle, "A New Appeal to the Old Whigs." He agrees with Lord Acton that "the notion of a higher law above municipal codes, with which Whiggism began, is the supreme achievement of Englishmen and their bequest to the nation," and, Hayek adds, "to the world." He writes that in "its pure form it is represented in the United States, not by the radicalism of Jefferson, nor by the conservatism of Hamilton or even John Adams, but by the ideas

---

[133] *The Constitution of Liberty*, p. 407.
[134] *Ibid.*, p. 407.
[135] *Wilhelm Tell*, Act II, scene 2.
[136] *The Constitution of Liberty*, pp. 168, 194-195.

of James Madison, the 'father of the Constitution.' "[137]
From this statement it can be concluded that Hayek, while he
believes in higher law as a constant guide for the improvement
of municipal law, and considers change according to higher law
justified for the sake of freedom, he is reluctant to accept
radical change. This is not surprising in a man who believes
that the large body of the law of an existing legal order has
grown gradually.

Difficult as it is to answer the question whether Hayek
favors revolution as a means for the absolute destruction of
an order characterized by the abuse of power and the absence
of the freedom of the individual, there is not much doubt
that his admission of the necessity of authority in a liberal
state, his emphasis upon the *constitution* of liberty, makes
him reluctant to want radical change in a society that is
predominantly liberal. He favors Madison, the great com-
promiser,[138] over Jefferson, Hamilton, and John Adams. For
the sake of order, he is willing to make compromises at the
cost of liberty, realizing that liberty, to be useful to men,
must be protected by a legal order.

In *The Road to Serfdom*, Hayek stated: "Within the known
rules of the game the individual is free to pursue his
personal ends and desires."[139] Known rules can restrict freedom. In 1953 Hayek voiced approval of Louis Philippe's
expressing ideas of Benjamin Constant according to which
liberty exists only under the law, and everybody must do
what the law requires.[140] His third Cairo lecture, entitled
"The Safeguards of Individual Liberty," was a lecture under
Ortega's motto, "Order is not a pressure imposed upon
society from without, but an equilibrium which is set up from
within." Here he first discusses "Law and Order" as a prerequisite for liberty, making plain that order does not exist

---

[137] *The Constitution of Liberty*, p. 409.
[138] Compare Alpheus T. Mason, *Free Government in the Making* (3rd ed., New York, 1965), pp. 189, 250-251, 312-313.
[139] *The Road to Serfdom*, p. 73.
[140] "Entstehung und Verfall des Rechtsstaatsideales," p. 49: "La liberté ne consiste que dans le règne des lois. Que chacun ne puisse être tenu de faire autre chose que ce que la loi exige de lui, et qu'il puisse faire tout ce que la loi n'interdit pas, telle est la liberté. C'est vouloir la détruire de vouloir autre chose."

merely as a result of human design, but also as a result of human action.[141] In *The Constitution of Liberty* Hayek devotes a chapter to "Responsibility and Freedom," writing: "Liberty and responsibility are inseparable. A free society will not function or maintain itself unless its members regard it as right that each individual occupy the position that results from his action and accept it as due to his own action. Though it can offer to the individual only chances and though the outcome of his efforts will depend on innumerable accidents, it *forcefully directs* his attention to those circumstances that he can control as if they were the only ones that mattered."[142] He continues with regret: "This belief in individual responsibility, which has always been strong when people firmly believed in individual freedom, has markedly declined, together with the esteem for freedom. Responsibility has become an unpopular concept, a word that experienced speakers or writers avoid because of the obvious boredom or animosity with which it is received by a generation that dislikes all moralizing." While responsibility "means an unceasing task, a discipline that man must impose upon himself if he is to achieve his aims,"[143] it also implies responsibility toward others. It means obedience to the laws. The latter idea is elaborated in the chapter, "Coercion and the State."[144] Finally, of his last work Hayek says: "The central concept around which the discussion of this book will turn is that of order.... Order is an indispensable concept.... We cannot do without it."[145]

The concessions the responsible unrepentant Old Whig is willing to make to the liberal order at the expense of freedom are manifold. They can be found with respect to individual rights and various concepts he believes to be conducive to liberty. They range from permitting the state to control weights and measures; to prevent fraud, deception, and vio-

---

[141] *The Political Ideal of the Rule of Law*, pp. 29-32. Compare Hayek's essay, "The Results of Human Action but not of Human Design."

[142] *The Constitution of Liberty*, p. 71. (Emphasis supplied.)

[143] *Ibid.*, pp. 71-72.

[144] *Ibid.*, pp. 133-147.

[145] *Rules and Order*, p. 35.

lence; and to make building regulations and factory laws;[146]
to allowing the state to tax individuals and require them to
do military service; all the way to the general right of the
government to build up an organization in order to preserve
internal peace and to keep out external enemies.[147]

Hayek believes that a spontaneous order is more conducive
to liberty than an imposed one. Yet, for the sake of order, he
refrains from denying that the latter and its laws should be
complied with.[148] The same applies to the law that comes
about through evolution and one that is the result of "reason:"[149] the law produced by human action and one produced by human design.[150] Hayek laments that during the
last generations, private law has been increasingly replaced by
public law, the former aiding, the latter threatening,
liberty.[151] Yet he does not urge disobedience to public law.
He complains that law in the sense of general rules is being
challenged by law in the sense of organizational orders.[152]
Yet, while he sees the latter as a danger to liberty, he does
not want it disobeyed. He feels that law based upon just
principles is better for freedom than law based upon expediency.[153] However, the latter must be obeyed. He distinguishes between *nomos*, the law of liberty, and *thesis*, the
law of legislation. There is no doubt about the former's
greater liberal content.[154] But Hayek wants the latter to be
complied with all the same.

The willingness to compromise at the cost of freedom does
not necessarily compromise freedom. On the contrary, it

---

[146] *The Road to Serfdom*, p. 81.

[147] *The Constitution of Liberty*, p. 143; *Rules and Order*, p. 124.

[148] *The Political Ideal of the Rule of Law*, pp. 29-32; *The Constitution of Liberty*, pp. 148-161; "Arten der Ordnung," p. 3; "Principles of a Liberal Social Order."

[149] "Principles of a Liberal Social Order"; *Rules and Order*, pp. 8-34.

[150] "The Results of Human Action but not of Human Design."

[151] *The Constitution of Liberty*, pp. 205-249; "Principles of a Liberal Social Order."

[152] *The Road to Serfdom*, pp. 72-87; *The Constitution of Liberty*, pp. 148-161; "Principles of a Liberal Social Order;" *Rules and Order*, pp. 94-144.

[153] "Die Ursachen der ständigen Gefährdung der Freiheit," p. 103; *Rules and Order* pp. 55-71.

[154] *Rules and Order*, pp. 94-144.

serves liberty by securing its protection through laws that reflect reason. "Though the sentiments which are expressed in such terms as the 'dignity of man' and the 'beauty of liberty' are noble and praiseworthy, they can have no place in an attempt at rational persuasion," he writes in the introduction to *The Constitution of Liberty*.[155] He wants to promote freedom rationally—through the law, the law of the state, the *Staatsrecht*. In doing so, the unrepentant Old Whig is an adamant advocate of law and order. He follows those who before him believed in the *Rechtsstaat* with its maximal realization of liberty. To Hayek, freedom ought to be the spirit of the laws, which alone can transform that spirit into true rights of man.

*Conclusion*

Hayek's ideas on the rule of law reveal him as a man of measure.

As we are close to the bicentennial of the publication of that seminal work, *The Wealth of Nations*, Hayek's legal thought reminds us not only of Montesquieu, but also of Adam Smith. The measure implied in the balance of powers made the great Frenchman, often considered the father of constitutionalism, famous. Measure is also characteristic of the great Scotsman, in whom many see the founder of political economy and economic liberalism. Like Hayek, Smith saw, as did Montesquieu, in the rule of law a means for the promotion of freedom. For Smith, justice implied the liberation of man from private as well as public oppression. Yet, despite his emphasis upon liberty, Smith is careful not to tend toward anarchy. He is convinced that the wealth of nations can be increased by the freedom of the individual rather than by his regulation and regimentation. At the same time, he admits controls here and there for what he considers the good of the society and its members. And he leaves no doubt that justice implies the protection of citizens from their fellow men through the government's enforcement of the laws.

Both Montesquieu and Smith had a great impact upon

---

[155] *The Constitution of Liberty*, p. 6.

the development in the United States. In her bicentennial celebrations, it seems proper to point out that the American Revolution, a continuation of the Whig revolution, was characterized by measure. Independence was declared on account of the excesses of monarchy. The Constitution was a reaction to democratic extremes. The founders' ideal was free government, a popular government under which the majority, while ruling, for the sake of the individual was limited by law which, for the citizen's safety, had to be strictly enforced. This was constitutionalism, which Hayek considers "The American Contribution."

Perhaps the liberal aristocrat who, in recognition of the lawful principle, *in dubio pro reo*, has, with *noblesse* and in good scholarly fashion, always given his opponents the benefit of the doubt; who gave his works mottoes from that man of measure, Goethe; who addressed *The Road to Serfdom* "to the socialists of all parties"; when he addressed *The Constitution of Liberty* to the unknown civilization that is growing in America, hoped that men would not lose measure and again respect the rule of law.

Shirley Robin Letwin

# The Achievement of
# Friedrich A. Hayek

Ours is an age of specialization—a lifetime is considered hardly enough to master one small corner of a discipline and only the bravest dare tread in other men's specialities. To find then a distinguished life's work as various as Hayek's is puzzling as well as impressive. And it is all the more so because the parts seem to be connected, and yet the character of the whole remains elusive. The oddity of it is well illustrated by one of Hayek's activities—his teaching at the University of Chicago, where for 12 years, from 1950, he was Professor of Social and Moral Science. The title was a strange one for a renowned economist. It belonged to another era when economists still cared to remember that Adam Smith had been a professor of moral philosophy, wrote a masterpiece called *The Theory of Moral Sentiments*, and had many distinguished successors who were notable philosophers.

Nevertheless Hayek more than justified his title and without anachronism. Every week he conducted a seminar of staggering catholicity. On Wednesdays after dinner, a large assortment of the wise and the callow, coming from all disciplines and all nations, assembled around a massive oval oak table in a mock Gothic chamber to talk about topics proposed by Hayek. They ranged, far from idly, across philosophy, history, social science, and knowledge generally. The seminar would have been distinguished if not otherwise by the senior participants: two atomic physicists, one an Italian holding a Nobel Prize, the other a Hungarian, profuse inventor of projects, physical, cinematic, political, and of every other sort; an Irish classicist and farmer, as completely master of Shakespeare, Gibbon, or Tolstoy, as of Sophocles, Plato, and Thucydides; a French Thomist of great piety and philosophical precision who admired Pascal, Proudhon, and T. S. Eliot;

147

an arch grass-roots American, founder of the Chicago School
of economists and a belligerent atheist with a passion for
theological inquiry; the leading monetary theorist, fascinated
by the sun-seeking motives of leaves on trees and the optimiz-
ing behaviors of economic actors, and game for any argument
that came his way; a classical archaeologist, educated in the
iconographic traditions of Munich and Berlin, who conducted classes on Nietzsche and tutorials on Proust; the
author of *The Gothic Cathedral* and the author of *The Lonely
Crowd*; as well as the inventor of the "folk society" and the
discoverer of early industrial revolutions. The students, drawn
from Japan, the Middle East, Europe, and outlying corners of
America, showed high promise of talents that would as
thoroughly defy classification.

   Hayek presided over this remarkable company with a gentle
rectitude that made his seminar an exercise in the liberal
virtues. Every remark, however fatuous, no matter how
obscure or young the speaker, was heard to the very end with
a respect that the weaker members found maddening. The
general subject was liberalism and no one was in any doubt
about Hayek's convictions. But students who hoped to shine
by discovering apostasy to an official creed learned to seek
other paths to glory. Hunting for the holy grail was definitely
out of order. The seminar was a conversation with the living
and the dead, ancient and modern; the only obligation was to
enter into the thoughts of others with fidelity and to accept
questions and dissent gracefully.

   Hayek's conduct as a colleague and teacher was entirely of
a piece with this impeccably liberal colloquium. When work
submitted by a student had been pronounced hopeless by
everyone else, Hayek could be relied on to wonder whether
perhaps it was not a work of genius that they had failed to
understand. Standards that have all but disappeared from
academic life were meticulously observed by him. About his
own research he had absolutely no sense of property. He was
never heard to claim credit; his collection of Mill's letters was
handed out to anyone interested and then casually handed
over to someone proposing to do a complete edition without
delay. Funds offered to him were not employed in the ortho-

dox manner for building a private empire; they were noise-lessly diverted to students and colleagues, to whom help came as if from an invisible hand.

The rest of Hayek's work is even more curious. What are we to make of someone who, on the one hand, denounces efforts to subject everything to "rational control" and remake men according to an ideal pattern while, on the other hand, he condemns deciding each question on its merits and produces *The Constitution of Liberty*, discussing the education of children, building regulations, subsidies to farmers, and conservation policies? How can we reconcile Hayek's admiration of individualism and innovation with his eulogies of traditions of thought and conduct? What connection is there between Hayek's mastery and admiration of scientific theory and his attention to the personal histories of men, carried to the point of following Mill's every footstep in Greece?

What connects all these seemingly contradictory parts is a particular understanding of the human world. It is a historical world of continuity as well as change, a world full of variety, in personalities and ideas as well as circumstances, achievements, and kinds of understanding. It did not begin yesterday or even with Adam Smith. It is not divided neatly between true believers and infidels. It is populated by Greeks and Romans, Frenchmen, Germans, and Englishmen, along with Austrians. Some lived in ancient times; others just the other day.

It is a world in which it is essential to pay careful attention to words. Thus Hayek has pointed out that the Greeks made a distinction between *cosmos* and *taxis* that moderns lost. Though Burke and Tocqueville appear to condemn the "individualism" that Adam Smith favored, in fact they used the word differently. The German conception of the "enlightenment" ignored a fundamental division between the French and the English.

It is a world in which the ideas men hold are complicated and develop unexpected connections. In Schiller's *Aesthetic Education* there is an echo of Milton's *Areopagitica*. A socialist may have no use for Marx. That a liberal flirts with Comte does not forever damn him, but requires explanation.

It is a world in which the uniqueness of each human personality must always be noticed. In telling us about the Saint Simonians, Hayek tells us also that Saint Simon sold the lead from the roofs of Notre Dame, organized a stage-coach service, manufactured Republican playing cards, and proposed to Mme. de Stael with the words: "As you are the most extraordinary woman on earth and I am the most extraordinary man. . . ." He tells us that Enfantin and Bazard are supposed to have asked Louis Philippe to hand over the Tuileries to them because they were the only legitimate power on earth. Hayek produces no neat packages of "movements" or "isms," nor does he deny that intelligent and good men may find bad ideas attractive. He does not hide the fact that when Comte expounded his positive philosophy, Alexander von Humboldt, whom Hayek admires, was in the audience, and that the most diverse people became attached to the Saint Simonians—George Sand, Balzac, and Hugo; Liszt and Berlioz; Heine had not been in Paris 24 hours before he came to sit among them. And even the old Goethe, who had warned Carlyle away from the Saint Simonians, spent a day trying to get to the bottom of their doctrines.

In short, far from reducing everything to one, throughout his work Hayek displays an unfailing sensitivity to the distinction between the historical and the logical connections of ideas, to the distinctiveness of each man's thought and personality.

It is typical of Hayek that when, at the founding of the Mont Pelerin Society, he was urging international collaboration based "on agreement on a common set of values," he proposed that instead of drawing up a "programme" it would be more effective to think of "some great figure who embodies in an especially high degree the virtues and ideals which such an association would have to serve. . . ."[1]

In part, Hayek's excursions into history were undoubtedly inspired by sheer love of learning. He is a kind of reader far from fashionable now. He has dawdled and browsed among books, and become so absorbed that he forgot what purpose

---

[1] *Studies in Philosophy, Politics, and Economics* (London, 1967), p. 142. (Referred to hereafter as *PPE*.)

brought him there. His historical studies are nevertheless linked to his interest in promoting a "regime of freedom" by his belief that men make their world in accordance with their understanding, and that this is a fundamental postulate of the liberalism he admires. He has long been aware, as few libertarians are as yet, of the irony of our current state of affairs where Marxists who deny the independence of ideas from things devote themselves assiduously to abstract subjects such as moral and legal philosophy, even metaphysics, which their opponents steadfastly disdain.

If liberalism is to be saved, Hayek has told us repeatedly, we must above all regain that "belief in the power of ideas" which "was the mark of liberalism at its best."[2] He has therefore directed much of his attention to the character of thought and knowledge. In doing so, he has moved very far away from some of the dreams that were entertained in the Vienna of his youth, the Vienna of Carnap and Freud. To have resisted such powerful intellectual fashions—which still dominate even those outside Vienna—is in itself remarkable. There is no one else who has done so as emphatically and consistently. Hayek has always denied, in a variety of contexts and arguments, the delusion that so captivated leading intellectuals in Vienna and their opponents as well as disciples throughout the world to this day—that there is a single touchstone or source of truth. And he has always insisted on sharply separating the life of the mind from the world of physical objects. He wrote *The Sensory Order* to show that there could not be a unified system of knowledge because mind "must remain forever a realm of its own, which we can know only through directly experiencing it, but which we shall never be able fully to explain or to 'reduce' to something else."[3]

What interests Hayek in human beings is their ability to do something more than pursue the satisfaction of given wants, to invent not only wants but also abstract ideas in order to understand themselves and their world. He himself has been

---

[2] *PPE*, p. 194.
[3] *The Sensory Order* (London, 1952), p. 194.

more concerned with discovering what different parts are played in human conduct by unselfconscious, spontaneously grown understanding and by deliberate, self-conscious thought. The picture of knowledge that emerges from his work is that of a vast and heterogeneous heritage produced by human experience over the years, out of which different parts have been selected from time to time to be self-consciously identified and explored. What is present to a man's consciousness represents only a minute portion of the ideas on which his thinking rests. Any understanding, whether of politics or of science, depends on a fund of habits, conventions, languages, and moral beliefs—what Hayek calls "unarticulated rules." This means that "articulated rules" do not spring full-blown from this or that man's head, but formulate an understanding which already exists and which will continue to give meaning to what has been self-consciously articulated. There are many degrees and varieties of self-consciousness and these are part of a whole well beyond what any man or number of men can grasp. To reduce the objects of legitimate belief to what has been made explicit in one manner, scientific or other, is to forgo civilization and embrace barbarism.

The moral that Hayek emphasizes is that civilization has been produced by cooperation—rather than struggle—between freedom and necessity. Moreover he attributes the necessity as well as the freedom to human rationality, and he argues that both bring us blessings as well as perils.

What others have taken to be necessity imposed on human beings by nonrational forces, Hayek has explained as the unintended consequences of their deliberate decisions. It is these unintended consequences that produce what Hayek calls a "spontaneous order." In a great many different contexts he has shown how an outcome that we find desirable may not have been designed by anyone; it may be an unforeseen consequence of measures taken by men of independent and even opposed purposes which together produced what no one intended. Similarly, some of the worst evils have been brought about neither by selfish interests nor by evil intentions but by honest convictions and good will. Though our ancestors acted deliberately and what followed is their doing, they need not, indeed could not, both for better and for worse, have foreseen our present state of affairs: for ideas may acquire unexpected connections. Individual actions and circumstances interact in unforeseen ways. The unselfconscious ideas that men have about what is possible and right decide much that goes unnoticed when deliberate decisions are taken. Thus what will come of our beliefs and actions may be very different from what we expect. And just as surely as we are constrained by the measures taken yesterday, what we do today will in part determine what can be done tomorrow.

But on the other hand, Hayek has emphasized that we act deliberately and can know something about the connections and consequences of ideas and actions. Any sane man tries to connect his ideas in some orderly fashion. And ideas have a certain intractability; they do not lend themselves equally well to all purposes. We are therefore responsible for what we think and do, and cannot absolve ourselves from reflecting on our thought and conduct. We can determine how we live if we have a firm grasp of what is entailed in the sort of life that we prefer. This does not mean that we try to decide everything. It means rather that we must understand both how much and how little we can, or should, deliberately decide. We must recognize that some matters are best settled by attending only to details, but that in other respects we can hope to grasp only the broad outline.

This is a subtle and complicated outlook and therefore uncommon. The first attempt to explicate it was made by David Hume, with whom Hayek rightly feels a special affinity. Whereas Hume came to this understanding through a painful acquaintance with the vices of Presbyterians, Hayek arrived at it by reflecting on the virtues of economists. The theory of economics shows that endlessly changing concrete choices made by endlessly changing men and women unintentionally produce a stable order. Hayek asked a question that an economist is not obliged to consider: What brings these two sorts of phenomena together? In other words, if we do not believe in that "invisible hand" that Adam Smith so

casually and unfortunately invoked and that economists talk
of all too often, what accounts for an order that has not been
deliberately designed?

His search for the answer led Hayek to recognize a new
predicament. As it is a newly identified predicament it is
easily confused with other more familiar ones. Hayek himself
has described some of the difficulties of his own enterprise:

> There can be few more thankless tasks at present than the essen-
> tial one of developing the philosophical foundation on which the
> further development of a free society must be based. Since the
> man who undertakes it must accept much of the framework of the
> existing order, he will appear to many of the speculatively minded
> intellectuals merely as a timid apologist of things as they are; at
> the same time, he will be dismissed by the men of affairs as an
> unpractical theorist. He is not radical enough for those who know
> only the world where "with ease together dwell the thoughts" and
> much too radical for those who see only how "hard in space
> together clash the things."[4]

It is easy to mistake Hayek's enterprise because of the
peculiar character of his objective. The title of *The Constitution of Liberty* might tempt one, for instance, to put it in the
class of "utopias," that strange brand of literature of which
Sir Thomas More is the acknowledged master and H. G. Wells
the last notable creator, a literature distinguished by its indifference to original sin and exaltation of the powers of reason.
And this seems a plausible classification because Hayek has
described himself as engaged in outlining a "liberal utopia."
Or else, Hayek's frequent insistence on the importance of
reasoning from "fixed principle," of devising a "program" for
a "regime of liberty," might suggest that he is a successor to
Bentham, who proposed to invent a "perfect system of legislation" suitable for all times and all places on "the grand
principle of utility." But Hayek is doing neither of these.

He is not pursuing a dream or elaborating an invention.
His concern with history, far from being an adventitious frill
of learning, is intrinsic to his purpose because his object is to
understand a way of living that is already known. He is not
answering the question, What is a free society? as if it were an

---

[4]*PPE*, p. 191.

abstraction beyond history for which he proposes to create a definition out of nothing. His question is rather: What are the precise characteristics of that which we have come to recognize as the life of free men? In other words, he is exploring a manner of living which others have over the years enjoyed and devised arrangements for protecting. But as the art of preserving and extending such arrangements has been lost or wantonly destroyed, Hayek set himself to recovering it. And it is the manner of making arrangements, not their content in the past, that Hayek wants to restore.

To see the originality of what Hayek has done, it is important to understand just why he thinks that this art has been lost. The predicament that he has diagnosed is novel because it does not consist simply in a lack of self-conscious understanding; it arises out of peculiar circumstances that make such an understanding imperative. Though Hayek is concerned with formulating principles, he is not in the least disposed to deprecate "muddling through." On the contrary, he recognizes in it a great gift of the English which until recently preserved an unbroken tradition of liberty. But Hayek has seen too the fragility of that gift and what has destroyed its efficacy.

"Muddling through" worked in the past, he has explained, not because Englishmen were indifferent to abstract ideas but because they had them so well in mind. Their political practice was based on such a firm understanding of what measures were permissible, that Englishmen "knew instinctively" what things "are not done," and could take decisions in a consistent manner without discussing premises and principles. The French talked so much about principles because they had no such "instinctive" understanding. They replaced it with principles and doctrines which they mistook for a higher exercise of reason but which only displayed their deficiencies more effectively. While pretending to be more clear-headed than the English, they produced revolution and destruction.

But though Hayek admires the old sort of "instinctive certainty," he carefully distinguishes it from what is now taken to be "judicious" behavior, that is, a refusal to consider the connection of particular decisions with any general ideas. Such disdain of all abstract reflection is often defended as the virtue of deciding each question "on its merits." Hayek considers such behavior reckless and destructive. If only for want of any other purpose, it reduces politics to a search for the satisfaction of current wants. The business of politicians is then supposed to consist in removing all sources of discontent. Each effort to do so inspires new discontents. And as dissatisfaction can never be completely removed from human life, the result of such expectations is an ever accelerating flow of new regulations. Then rules of law are replaced by administrative orders, stable expectations become impossible, and liberty is destroyed. Thus by myopically pursuing immediate benefits, those who judge each question "on its merits" shape a social order devoid of what matters most to them.

It is no less disastrous to replace the old sort of "instinctive certainty" with an addiction to "moderation." Hayek has criticized conservatives not, as some libertarians wrongly suppose, for respecting tradition, but for not knowing what they respect. They have no coherent understanding which could give them grounds for ordering alternatives and connecting their choices. They consequently have no steady way of judging policies. Lacking an "instinct" for what things "are not done," and having acquired no self-conscious understanding to replace it, they disguise their confusion by bogus appeals to "tradition," or more fashionably now, to "moderation." But the man who knows only that the truth must lie somewhere between the extremes, knows only shadows. He is obliged to shift his position "every time a more extreme movement appears on either wing."[5] And so the conservative in pursuit of moderation becomes but a paler reflection of the most fashionable revolutionaries.

Nor is this unhappy condition confined to those who profess conservatism. What has impressed Hayek is that for some time now, almost all would-be lovers of liberty have been reduced to confusion. He has found in Tocqueville's account of the timeless limbo inhabited by Americans part of the explanation. The continual movement characteristic of modern democratic communities has weakened or broken the ties

---

[5] *The Constitution of Liberty* (Chicago, 1960), p. 399.

between one generation and the next, so that men have lost track of the ideas of their forefathers. At the same time, they are being constantly exposed to new ideas. And while they are blinded by this sandstorm in the desert, they are attacked by enemies of liberty, who come armed with sharp blueprints and automatic doctrines and are aggressive and self-confident.

Though it is peculiarly troublesome now, this predicament diagnosed by Hayek might arise wherever affairs have been arranged by an "instinctive" practice. It will appear once men who have slowly and unself-consciously developed satisfactory ways of doing things are compelled to produce public justification for their beliefs and conduct by opponents who have been drilled in Sunday schools run by apostles of utopia. To deal with such opponents, one has to have struggled with the arguments that may be brought against one's own beliefs, learned to think of possible objections and of how to answer them. But those who have learned certain ways of understanding and doing things by apprenticeship are quickly made all too aware of how much gets lost when they try to spell out their knowledge. Never having engaged in the exercise, they lack the skill even to make the attempt.

Our current obsession with equality has made this predicament especially severe. Politics is no longer the business only of those directly engaged in it. Men of no experience, talent, or even interest in politics feel obliged or are pressed to hold political opinions even on matters of fine detail. These amateur politicians have not learned the art of deliberating about what is likely to be desirable and feasible. Instead they have learned to despise deference to older and wiser heads, and to venerate only the "scientific" mode of thought or what they take for it. They are not therefore impressed by anything so amorphous as a sense for "what is not done," slow procedures, and intricate arguments, but rather by numbers and diagrams, by formulas and doctrines, by anything that gives quick, complete answers and banishes the discomforts of uncertainty and complexity. Nor is this disease confined to politics. It has infected every aspect of life from schools to marriage. Every practice and every institution is now being attacked by men of the book, newly arrived men

with no sense for nuance to disturb their certainties. Against
such vulgar and cunning adventurers even those who still
know instinctively what is not done cannot summon the
words for a convincing reply.

Thanks to such developments what is left of the unself-
conscious practice of liberalism has become confused. If
change moved more slowly and men were more patient, these
confusions might in time have become untangled in the same
unself-conscious fashion. But as issues have multiplied rapidly
and have had to be settled quickly, men of good will have
fallen into supporting what they believe themselves to oppose.

Much of Hayek's labor has accordingly been devoted to
discovering and untangling such insidious confusions. He has
attacked, for example, our current addiction to talk of "social
justice" and "social conscience," which socialists regularly
brandish as their most formidable weapon. But he has not just
attacked it. He has pointed out that the talk of "social
justice" may be inspired by dissatisfaction with a free enterprise system for rewarding men according to their services,
rather than their moral merit. It is "neither honest nor effective," Hayek says, to deny this discrepancy or its unsatisfac-
toriness. Instead liberals have to make clear why these draw-
backs are nevertheless preferable to those of other alternatives.[6] Besides, Hayek shows that adding the adjective "social" to the simple old words of "justice" and "conscience"
implicitly denies both the supremacy of the rule of law and
the recognition of individual responsibility, thus making justice impossible and conscience meaningless.[7] In similar fashion, he has reminded us that when we speak of a "value to
society," what is in question is the value of some services to
certain people, and that the conception of a "value to society" is "in a free order as illegitimate an anthropomorphic
term as the description of 'one economy,' in the strict sense,
as an entity which 'treats' people justly or unjustly, or 'distri-
butes' among them."[8] Hayek has given us enough of such

---

[6] *PPE*, p. 233.
[7] *PPE*, pp. 237ff.
[8] *PPE*, p. 172.

observations for a comprehensive dictionary of liberal mal-apropisms.

Not only careless confusion, Hayek has found, but also a misguided pursuit of clarity has bedevilled would-be libertarians. Feeling themselves at bay, they have grasped at simple prescriptions. They have as a result become attached to irrelevant accretions and turned their beliefs into a rigid creed. Then, when they are confronted with proposals which their ill-conceived position forbids them to consider but to which they cannot discover any objections, they are tempted to desert their own good sense by staying with their creed. Or else, having acknowledged that the program of those whom they took for enemies includes some desirable measures, they assume that the rest must be equally harmless and so they sell the pass.

In this way, ignorance of the abstract ideas on which the practice of living as free men rests has destroyed liberty. The practice of freedom therefore no longer can be preserved unself-consciously. Yet an addiction to organizing things according to programs has destroyed liberty. This is the predicament that Hayek has over many years, through many pages and in a great variety of contexts, so painstakingly traced.

The remedy that he has suggested is even more easily mistaken than the disease he has diagnosed. The self-consciousness that Hayek wishes to promote is of a difficult sort. It is so unusual because it is inspired not by an intoxication with blueprints, but by the reluctant discovery that when unself-conscious knowledge of the life of free men is threatened by men of the book, there is no hope of enjoying freedom without anatomizing it. Hayek has done this by formulating what he describes as "principles" of a liberal social order.

But these are not, as other men's principles are, patterns with which the arrangements we make have to agree. Neither are they universal laws that can enable us to predict what has not yet happened. Nor are they designed to serve as axioms from which certainties about what to do can be deduced. They do not propose to give us a destination, but a map of the territory in which we find ourselves. They are general considerations discovered by reflecting on a manner of arranging our affairs which once prevailed and is now only dimly remembered. They are criteria for judging whether proposals made to us are hostile to that manner of conducting ourselves or will help us to enjoy it more fully. They are what Hume called maxims, that is, generalizations about what is "true only of most but not of all instances."[9] In short, Hayek's principles promise no escape from uncertainty. They offer only to mitigate incoherence.

To seek coherence without pursuing certainty is a most delicate enterprise. The predicament that Hayek's principles are meant to relieve may all too easily be aggravated by saying too much, in the wrong way, at the wrong time. And far from belittling the dangers of straying into that "constructivist rationalism" he has so roundly condemned, Hayek has repeatedly pointed out such dangers in a number of different connections. Libertarians may disagree with Hayek on many issues which would not for a moment surprise or disturb him. But those who disagree with him on these matters would do well to think again about what they mean by libertarianism.

It was a joke of his youth, Hayek has told us, that Austrian economists were superior to the German ones because the Austrians had no influence on practical affairs. "I have later observed," Hayek says, "the same difference between the English and American economists; at least in the 30's, the English economists were undoubtedly the better theoreticians and at the same time much less involved in the conduct of current policy. This has somewhat changed since, and I am not sure that the effect has been altogether beneficial for the state of scientific economics in England." And about his own work, Hayek has said: "If I have succeeded . . . in building up something like a fairly systematic body of opinion on economic policy that is not least due to the circumstance that all this time I had to be content with the role of a spectator and had never to ask what was politically possible or would assist any group with which I was connected."[10]

[9] *PPE*, p. 264.
[10] *PPE*, pp. 265-266.

Hayek is not advocating an eternal ban against political talk by economists, but a recognition of the proper relation between abstract understanding and practical decisions. The distinction between them is essential to liberalism, which springs from a respect for concrete knowledge. An abstract theory cannot be used for deciding political issues without determining what conditions in the real world "correspond" to the theoretical scheme. And this, Hayek points out, is often more difficult than understanding the theory itself. It requires a skill rather different from the economist's, "something like a sense for the physiognomy of events."[11] Therefore while economic theory can tell us a great deal about "the effectiveness of different kinds of economic systems," it has "comparatively little to say on the concrete effects of particular measures in given circumstances. . . ."[12]

By the same token the politician who speaks as an economist fails at his job. The politician's concern is with what is practicable in the existing state of opinion. He will be irresponsible and dangerous if he pursues policies without any sense for their relation to more general beliefs about what is possible and desirable. But if he commits himself to policies as if they were laws of nature, he may as easily be destructive and he is certain to become obsolescent.

Both politicians and economists must beware of confusing what may legitimately be said in the abstract with what can only be decided at a given time and place. Those who try to define in the abstract the concrete aims of government may soon find themselves "having to oppose state action which appears to have only desirable consequences" or "having to admit that they have no general rule on which to base their objections to measures which, though effective for particular purposes, would in their aggregate effect destroy a free state."[13] While those who wish to contribute to a general understanding must emancipate themselves from "that servitude in which the politician is held," anyone out to give

[11]*PPE*, p. 129.
[12]*PPE*, p. 263.
[13]*The Constitution of Liberty*, p. 258.

practical advice "must take a sane view of what persuasion and instruction are likely to achieve."[14]

This distinction between abstract understanding and practical decisions makes it impossible to promote liberalism with formulas. The disposition to make "the absence of state activity" the foundation of liberalism, Hayek has said, must bear an important responsibility for the decline of competition and the success of socialism. The traditional discussions of liberalism have done great damage by suggesting that once the principles of private property and freedom of contract are recognized, all issues are settled, "as if the law of property and contract were given once and for all in its final and most appropriate form."[15] In fact there never has been and probably could not be a legal system that "leaves the kind of contractual obligations on which the order of society rests entirely to the ever new decision of the contracting parties."[16]

For all that Hayek has said about the virtues of the market as a "spontaneous order," he has taken just as great pains to dispose of the fantasy of "laissez-faire" conjured up by that "invisible hand" and to explain that the "spontaneous order" of the market is not a mechanical process given by nature. It consists, Hayek steadily reminds us in one fashion or other, of men buying and selling, investing and managing under special historical conditions. Such activities can produce desirable unintended consequences, but they will not necessarily do so. That will depend on the procedures governing those activities. And these have to be set by us, in accordance with our purposes and our conceptions of how we can best achieve them. One of Hayek's greatest contributions to the defense of liberty is his repeated assertion that belief in the free market and competition, far from absolving us of having to think of legal arrangements, obliges us to do so more carefully. The art of making social arrangements that Hayek would recover for us consists in attending with meticulous deliberation to some things while letting others arrange themselves.

---

[14] *Individualism and Economic Order* (London, 1949), pp. 108f.

[15] *Individualism*, p. 111.

[16] *Individualism*, p. 115.

And when we are thinking about deliberate arrangements, we cannot, Hayek emphasizes, escape decisions about what is "just." The rule of law, as Hayek understands it, does not consist merely in a set of rules; it is a system of just rules. Hayek has had some pungent things to say about the attempts of positivists to sterilize our thinking of moral ideas. A good deal more attention should be paid to that. Hayek was never seduced by the hope of substituting purely formal criteria for moral judgments in the law, held out by Kelsen and his followers: "a conception of the rule of law which merely demands that a command be legitimately issued and not that it be a rule of justice equally applicable to all (what the Germans called the merely *formelle Rechtsstaat*) of course no longer provides any protection for individual freedom."[17]

In all these ways, far from encouraging us to simplify political deliberation, Hayek's exploration of the principles of "a regime of freedom" is designed to inhibit such attempts. He has no use for the popular, brutal opposition between "freedom" and "power." Instead he has meticulously distinguished different sorts of constraints. For the choice before human beings, as he understands them, is only between different kinds of constraint. The liberal prefers the constraints imposed by the rule of law. What matters then is to be quite clear about the character of different kinds of social arrangements. And the central distinction for Hayek is that between more and less abstract constraints. By exploring the implications of this distinction he has shown how it is possible to order the whole without suppressing or losing sight of the concrete diversity that constitutes a rich civilization.

A most important implication of the liberal preference for abstract constraints, to which Hayek has paid a good deal of attention, is that moral traditions should be cherished, not destroyed; the order of a moral practice is even more abstract than that imposed by rules of law. Because it consists in a steady manner of choosing rather than in a set of rules, a moral practice saves us from being a jumble of responses without preventing us from adjusting our actions finely to

---

[17]*PPE*, pp. 169ff.

changing circumstances. Moreover, a firmly established moral practice enables us to dispense with rules of law in large areas of our life. In addition, it is our source for the rules that we do need. Therefore, if we destroy moral traditions, we destroy "the indispensable bases of a free civilization. . . ."[18]

The disposition to reject moral rules "whose utility is not rationally demonstrated," Hayek has condemned as part of the same rationalist frame of mind that makes it impossible to understand how the market can order economic activities.[19] Though he has drawn his understanding of an abstract order from economic theory, he has never lost sight of how the economist's theoretical world differs from the real one. He has concluded rather that the better we understand the interaction between the deliberately arranged and the spontaneously grown aspects of social order, of which economics discloses one aspect, the more clearly we come to see that real men and women are not, as the economist's abstractions are, interchangeable units with no other definite or durable relations to one another than those that occur in the course of maximizing utilities. Moreover, Hayek has made a point of warning us, as Burke and Tocqueville had before, that to the degree that we destroy all implicit common ties and conventions and succeed in reducing individuals to isolated bundles of wants and satisfactions, such as the economist postulates, we are issuing an invitation to the sort of centralized tyranny that the libertarian is supposed to abhor.

The view that individualism is based on "isolated or self-contained individuals instead of starting from men whose whole nature and character is determined by their existence in society,"[20] has been flatly condemned by Hayek as "the silliest of common misunderstandings." In his essay on "Individualism: True and False" he has told us of how astonished he was, as a student, by the behavior of the English as they then were. Their country was famed for its individualism and liberty, and yet they were "disposed to

---

[18] *Individualism*, p. 25.

[19] *Individualism*, p. 24.

[20] *Individualism*, p. 6.

conform in all externals to common usage rather than as seemed natural to me, to be proud to be different and original in most respects." Instead it was the Germans who took great pains to "develop an original personality" which in every respect expressed what he had come to regard as right and true. But Hayek came to see this as a "false individualism" which contributed to the German failure to develop a sound regime of freedom, and disposed them to accept from a totalitarian state the order that they could not find for themselves.[21]

This false individualism became fashionable in England too. Keynes described its earliest manifestations in Bloomsbury:

> We repudiated entirely customary morals, conventions, and traditional wisdom. We were, that is to say, in the strict sense of the term, immoralists. The consequences of being found out had, of course, to be considered for what they were worth. But we recognized no moral obligation on us, no inner sanction to conform or to obey. Before heaven we claimed to be our own judge in our own case. . . .[22]

The claim to self-sufficiency, the lack of deference to what others thought and did in the past, the certainty of a self-appointed coterie of elect displayed in this credo is a far cry from the "true individualism" described by Burke in a statement that Hayek admires:

> Men are qualified for civil liberty in exact proportion to their disposition to put moral chains upon their appetites; in proportion as their love of justice is above their rapacity; in proportion as their own soundness and sobriety of understanding is above their vanity and presumption; in proportion as they are more disposed to listen to the councils of the wise and good, in preference to the flattery of the knaves.[23]

A sad confirmation of Hayek's distinction is seen now in England where the progress of "false individualism" has been accompanied by a rush to embrace serfdom.

It follows from his respect for an individualism that recognizes its dependence on a moral and intellectual inheritance

---

[21] *Individualism*, p. 26.

[22] *PPE*, pp. 89f.

[23] "A Letter to a Member of the National Assembly," *Works* (World's Classics), IV, p. 319 quoted in *Individualism*, p. 24.

that Hayek should distinguish education from technical training. His sense for the difference between them should be
noticed especially by economists of his persuasion. They may
talk seductively of variety and freedom but when it comes to
education their rationalist, constructivist hoof is bound to
show. The rationalist has no use for established disciplines and
procedures. He disdains history and the arts, indeed anything
but science or something whose usefulness he can demonstrate. He will care only to impart technical information, by
means of techniques, in order to make technicians. He knows
the one road to truth, and he can lay it all out in black on
white.

Hayek has pointed out that technicians need to be shown
their niche in the production line. Free men who can make
their lives for themselves need something other than the latest
information about how to solve problems, how to do, or
make, or know this or that. They must have learned to
distinguish and appreciate the peculiar kind of consciousness
that can enable them to be critical of incoherent thought
without reducing the world to the dimensions of their own
finite minds. And they can do this only if they have acquired
an understanding of their past, of the disciplines and institutions developed by civilized men to teach them how to
deliberate and to discriminate, to order their imaginations in a
steady manner.

Hayek has accordingly advocated that specialization should
be preceded by a good general education, what used to be
called an education in the liberal arts. Far from sanctioning
the supermarket view of universities that would have them
purvey whatever the customers demand, an idea that other
"free market" economists find beguiling, he has denied that
all recognized research specialities are equally suitable as a
basic training, because only "certain kinds of specialization
deserve the name of 'disciplines' in the original sense of a
discipline of the mind."[24] What matters is learning "standards" and "what real competence is," and acquiring "the
conscience of a scholar."[25] Instead of identifying education

[24]*PPE*, p. 126.
[25]*PPE*, p. 125.

with the acquisition of scientific truth, he has deplored the isolation of the so-called social sciences from other disciplines and suggested that the study of literature and the arts might be quite as indispensable as the study of science. He has told economists, "He who is only an economist cannot be a good economist."[26] He has told social scientists generally, "If we are not to become a mainly destructive element, we must also be wise enough to understand that we cannot do without beliefs and institutions whose significance we do not understand and which, therefore, may seem meaningless to us. . . ."[27]

Thus patiently and meticulously Hayek has charted the varieties of submission that make men free. Though he has produced something that might be described as a doctrine or ideology of liberalism, he has given liberals neither catchwords nor solutions. He has shown that to remain free we must keep moving between an abstract understanding of the fundamental postulates of our thought and concrete practical knowledge. And he has required us to rejoice in the difficulties of maintaining such a precarious balance: for it goes with recognizing that a human being is a unique rational consciousness in a world where nothing stands still. And it is only for beings of this kind that liberty can matter. In short, Hayek has set lovers of liberty the most difficult of assignments—to think clearly about how to arrange our affairs without supposing that we can get to the root of all things or foresee all consequences. That requires a rare combination of diffidence, courage, and thoughtfulness. But then Hayek has also provided the model.

---

[26] *PPE*, p. 123.
[27] *PPE*, p. 130.

# Appendixes

Arthur Shenfield

# Friedrich A. Hayek: Nobel Prizewinner

When Professor Hayek (as the English-speaking world, where he spent thirty-one of his most fruitful years, generally calls him) was a young man he was uncertain whether to become an economist or a psychologist. He chose to be an economist, and as a result he has now received in some measure the recognition of high scholarly eminence in the form of the Nobel Prize for economics, which he long ago richly deserved—and deserved to receive without sharing it with, of all people, Gunnar Myrdal. Yet without a doubt he could have become a psychologist of equal eminence; and indeed, even though he would then have claimed to be no more than an amateur in psychology, he published in 1952 a book on the nature of sensory perception (*The Sensory Order*) which ranked with the works of psychologists of the highest professional standing.

Equally remarkable is the fact that for the greater part of the past 20 years, Hayek's main interest and main field of publication has not been economics but fundamental political theory (including, in recent years, fundamental legal theory). Thus it is that what is perhaps his greatest work (*The Constitution of Liberty*) is in the latter field, though of course there is much in it which could not have been written except by a political philosopher who was also an economist. It is a work which will rank imperishably among the classics of political philosophy. Since Hayek's perception of the nature of political society is in a direct line of descent from that of the specifically British scholars of the Enlightenment, no doubt Locke and Hume, Smith and Burke, are now looking down on him from the Heaven reserved for such men and marveling that out of Vienna there has sprung a thinker of their own

Adapted from an article published in *Criticon*, November 1974. Reprinted by permission.

sterling stamp, while the politicians and most of the scholars of their own now distressed country have long ago strayed far from the path that they opened up. So too, no doubt, is he being viewed with admiration by Acton, who was as much a Continental as an Englishman, and by de Tocqueville who, though in every respect a true Frenchman, was signally different from the thinkers of the French Enlightenment, among whom Hayek finds the essential source of the leading intellectual errors of our time. It need hardly be said that it is these intellectual errors which Hayek sees as the root of the destructive totalitarian tendencies of the twentieth-century world.

There is a further unexpected feature of Hayek's career. To anyone who knows him personally, as well as his publications, Hayek must appear to be the very embodiment of the cloistered scholarly virtues. Calm, reflective, interested above all in ideas, and standing apart from the rough and tumble which now characterizes the academic world almost as much as the worlds of politics and business, he would be the last person to be found caught up in anything that smacked of a "movement." Yet in the Mont Pelerin Society he founded something which may indeed become a "movement"—a danger which has occasionally induced him to contemplate its winding up. As its president from 1947 to 1960 (when he was succeeded by the late Professor Roepke) and its honorary president since then, he has been its inspiration and guiding light from the beginning. He has always thought of the Society, and always striven to maintain it, as a company of scholars, exchanging and developing their ideas in mutual intercourse but in no way seeking to make propaganda. His first thought, when casting about for a name for the Society, was to call it the Acton-Tocqueville Society, which indicates its intellectual inspiration. He has succeeded. The Mont Pelerin Society remains a forum for scholarly intercourse, no more and no less. Yet, since the academic world is almost everywhere in the grip of ideas hostile to those of the members of the Mont Pelerin Society, those who thus suffer intellectual discomfort have tended to seek the scholarly shelter of the Society, which now has some 350 members spread through 33 countries and which could have many more if it opened its doors wide to receive them.

Hence the Society tends to be tugged in the direction of becoming an academic pressure group, especially as some of its members are as successful in popular economic debate as in contributing to the advancement of their science in the learned economic journals. Thus the fact that the Society has so far continued to bear Hayek's very special stamp of academic detachment is testimony to the integrity of his character.

Hayek's career has four phases. He was born in Vienna in 1899, the son of a professor of botany at the University. Thus he was just old enough to glimpse the charm of the Austrian civilization which died in World War I. From 1927 to 1931 he was director of the Austrian Institute for Economic Research and from 1929 to 1931 lecturer in economics at the University of Vienna, where he taught in the tradition of Menger, Wieser, Böhm-Bawerk and Mises.

In 1931 he was invited to take a Chair at the London School of Economics where he stayed until 1950, becoming in 1938 a naturalized British subject, which he still is. In England, between the World Wars, he found still alive many of the admirable features of the pre-1914 civilization which had already departed from Austria, though obviously even in England the seeds of decay had been sown.

In 1950 he accepted an offer to take a Chair at the University of Chicago, the most celebrated center in the United States of scholars championing the free market economy and the free society of which that economy is the shield and support. There he stayed until 1962, when he entered his fourth phase by returning to German-speaking territory. From 1962 to 1969 he held a Chair at Freiburg i. B., the academic home of the late Professor Eucken and his neo-liberal followers, than which no other place in Germany could have been more congenial to him. Retiring in 1969, he came back to his native Austria, where he now teaches as a visiting professor at the University of Salzburg.

Hayek's scholarly work (apart from his contribution to psychology mentioned above) falls into three main parts: first, pure economic theory; second, problems of economic policy; third, fundamental political philosophy and legal theory.

His earliest works in economic theory were *Monetary*

*Theory and the Trade Cycle* (published in German in 1929, in English in 1933), and *Prices and Production* (1931). In *Monetary Theory and the Trade Cycle* he applied the insights into the monetary system successfully developed in Vienna, notably by Mises, to the phenomenon of economic fluctuations; and in *Prices and Production* he sought to apply to the same phenomenon the well-known Austrian concepts of round-aboutness and variations in the period of production.

In the monetary field it is perhaps hard for us now to realize how strong the grip then was in the German-speaking world of nonsensical monetary notions, without which the great German and Austrian inflations could not have happened. In the academic world the grip of these notions was exemplified by the high repute accorded such works as Georg Knapp's *State Theory of Money* and perhaps even more by the fact that Knapp was thought to be a liberal. In this, as in other fields, the economists' Vienna was an island of sense and analytical penetration in a sea of confusion.

Of these two works *Monetary Theory and the Trade Cycle* was probably the more successful; but neither was wholly successful, which is understandable when one bears in mind that they were written before the great explosion of academic disputation on the trade cycle and the problem of unemployment in the 1930s. *Prices and Production* bore the marks of compression inevitable in the lectures from which it was compiled, which made it possible for critics to drive some holes through its exposition; and of course its ideas were soon swamped by the tide of Keynesianism.

After further work rooted in Austrian concepts, but displaying modifications, Hayek published in 1941 a work which has claims to a place among the finest studies in economic theory, namely *The Pure Theory of Capital*. In penetration and comprehensiveness this was a masterpiece which, though still saluted by specialists in capital theory, has nevertheless never made the full impact that it merited. By 1941, and during the decade or two thereafter, Keynes had conquered the academic world, and little attention was paid to ideas of different provenance.

During this period Hayek was also concerned with problems

of economic policy, though of course his theoretical work also obviously had a bearing on policy. He wrote little of full-length character in this field, but his contribution as editor to *Collectivist Economic Planning* (1935) was notable. This was the work that developed Mises' pathbreaking demonstration of the problem of calculation facing every centrally planned economy, which no central planner, or theoretical economist, has ever solved. Also *Monetary Nationalism and International Stability* (1937) was a warning of the grave consequences of the breakup of the international monetary order which began in 1931.

The third group of works begins with *Scientism and the Study of Society* (1942-44 in *Economica*, later published in 1952 in *The Counter-Revolution of Science*), and goes on through *The Road to Serfdom* (1944), *Individualism and Economic Order* (1948), *The Constitution of Liberty* (1960), plus several other subsidiary books, to culminate in the latest work which is still in progress, *Law, Legislation and Liberty* (Volume 1, 1974).

In the same period Hayek edited, and contributed to, the famous essays (arising out of papers read at a Mont Pelerin Society meeting) in *Capitalism and the Historians* (1954). These essays painstakingly refuted the errors of the novelists, journalists, and biased or inferior historians who propagated the widespread belief that early capitalism ground the worker down into misery. That the belief dies hard shows how powerful a grip myth of this kind can acquire on the public mind.

*Scientism and the Study of Society* is a superb analysis of the errors which arise from the attempt to apply the concepts and methods of the natural sciences to the social sciences. *The Road to Serfdom* is the famous essay which warned the world that centralized economic planning would inevitably lead to the end of the liberal society which was Europe's, indeed mankind's, highest social achievement. Since it was a tract for the general reader, did not Hayek here abandon the stance of the scholar in favor of that of the propagandist, so out of character for him? The answer is NO. If the word "propaganda" be given the non pejorative sense which is its due as much as is the pejorative sense, the tract was indeed propaganda. Yet it is in every line a work of scholarship, as evidenced by some who did not agree with it, notably the late Professor Schumpeter.

It is true that there is a sense in which the western world, to which it was addressed, has by-passed its warnings. For it foresaw the downward slide to serfdom as the specific result of centralized economic planning, and if the West had persisted with such planning, so dear to the "intellectuals" of Hayek's time of writing, we should almost certainly have by now reached the end of that road. Instead we have taken the road of inflation, governmental profligacy, and uncoordinated governmental intervention into the market; and this must lead us to the serfdom that Hayek foresaw just as certainly as centralized planning, if perhaps more slowly. Indeed, since uncoordinated governmental intervention can lead only to chaos, it will itself produce a clamor for true central planning, unless forestalled by the re-education of the public, and thus bring us to serfdom by Hayek's original road.

The later works are essentially of one piece. They argue, in marvelously fair, temperate, penetrating and comprehensive manner, four basic propositions.

*First,* that the institutions which are the warp and woof of society arise from human action but not from human design; and hence that attempts to design society are fatal to its goodness.

*Second,* that in a free society law is essentially found, not made; so that it is not normally the mere will of the rulers, be they kings or democratic majorities.

*Third,* that the Rule of Law not only is the first and foremost principle of the free society, but also is dependent upon the two conditions set out above.

*Fourth,* that the Rule of Law requires men to be treated equally, but not only does not require them to be made equal but is undermined by attempts to do so.

Few other scholars, if any, have adorned the social sciences in our time as Hayek has done. It was time for the Nobel Prize Committee to recognize his eminence.

# A Selected List of Hayek's Books in English Currently in Print

*Prices and Production*, Augustus M. Kelley ($10)

*Monetary Theory and the Trade Cycle*, Augustus M. Kelley ($11.50)

*Collectivist Economic Planning*, Augustus M. Kelley ($12.50)

*Monetary Nationalism and International Stability*, Augustus M. Kelley ($7.50)

*Profits, Interest and Investment*, Augustus M. Kelley ($12.50)

*The Pure Theory of Capital*, University of Chicago Press ($16.00 paper)

*The Road to Serfdom*, University of Chicago Press ($8.00, $3.95 paper)

*Individualism and Economic Order*, Henry Regnery Company ($2.95 paper)

*The Counter-Revolution of Science*, The Free Press ($7.95)

*The Sensory Order: An Inquiry into the Foundations of Theoretical Psychology*,
  University of Chicago Press ($8.50 paper)

*Capitalism and the Historians*, University of Chicago Press ($6.00, $2.95 paper)
  (Edited and Introduction)

*The Constitution of Liberty*, University of Chicago Press ($12.50)
  (Henry Regnery Company, $3.95 paper)

*Studies in Philosophy, Politics and Economics*, University of Chicago
  Press ($12.00) (Touchstone-Clarion Imprint, Simon & Schuster, $2.95 paper)

*Law, Legislation and Liberty*, University of Chicago Press
  Volume I, *Rules and Order* ($8.50)
  Volume II, *The Mirage of Social Justice* (fall 1976)
  Volume III, *The Political Order of a Free Society* (in preparation)

Addresses of the publishers listed above:

University of Chicago Press, 5801 Ellis Avenue, Chicago, Illinois 60637

The Free Press, 866 Third Avenue, New York, New York 10022

Augustus M. Kelley, 300 Fairfield Road, Fairfield, New Jersey 07006

Henry Regnery Company, 180 North Michigan Avenue, Chicago, Illinois 60601

Simon & Schuster, 630 Fifth Avenue, New York, New York 10020

These books can be ordered from the Hillsdale College Bookstore (Hillsdale, Michigan 49242 USA). Please enclose payment with your order and add postage: $1.00 per book in USA, $2.00 per book outside USA.

The Institute for Humane Studies, 1177 University, Menlo Park, California 94025 has the following pamphlets by Hayek for sale at 50¢ each postpaid: "The Use of Knowledge in Society," "The Intellectuals and Socialism," "Kinds of Order in Society," and "The Rule of Law."

# Index

Hamilton, Alexander, 141, 142
Hammond, Barbara and J. L., 88
Hansen, Alvin, 18
Harrington, James, 118, 140
Harris, Ralph, xxiii
Hartwell, Ronald Max, vi, xxiv, 83, 90
Havender, William N., xxiii
Hawtrey, Sir Ralph, 18
Hazlitt, Henry, 109
Heckscher, August, 84
Hegel, Georg, 43, 61, 62, 124, 140
Heine, Heinrich, 150
Henshaw, Nancy, xix
Hicks, Sir John, 18, 27, 28, 32
Hitler, Adolph, 132
Hobhouse, Leonard Trelawney, 61, 62
Hoff, Ole Jacob, xxiv
Holdsworth, William S., 116
Holland, Philemon, 118
Howard, John A., xxiv
Hugo, Victor 150
Humboldt, Alexander von, 150
Hume, David, 43, 95, 109, 115, 126, 130, 133, 153, 160, 171
Hunold, Albert, 109
Hutt, William H., xxiv, 73

*Individualism and Economic Order*, 34, 88, 93, 162, 164, 165, 175
Institute for Humane Studies, 133
*Intellectuals and Socialism*, 77, 86, 88, 96

Jackson, Henry M., 103
James I of England, 119
Jefferson, Thomas, 141, 142
Jellinek, George, 140
Jevons, W. Stanley, 68
Jhering, Rudolf von, 114
Johnson, Lyndon, 115
Johnson, Malcolm, xix
Jouvenel, Bertrand de, 73, 74

Kaldor, Nicholas, 28, 32
Kant, Immanuel, 50, 114, 115, 133
Kelsen, Hans, 131, 138, 163
Kelvin, Lord, 67
Kemp, Arthur, xxiii
Kern, Fritz, 125
Keynes, John Maynard, 18, 25, 79, 96, 165, 174
Kirk, Russell, 103
Kirzner, Israel M., xxiv
Klingender, F. D., 79
Knäpp, Georg, 174
Knievel, Evel, 103

Knight, Frank H., 31
Kristol, Irving, 97

Ladd, Everett Carl, 87
Lange, Oskar, 34, 35
Laski, Harold, J., 88
Lawrence, D. H., 79
*Law, Legislation, and Liberty, Vol. I, Rules and Order, see also Rules and Order*, 1, 65, 76, 108, 109, 117, 120, 121, 123, 124, 133, 135, 175
Leoni, Bruno, 44, 136
*Les Prix Nobel, 1974*, xv
Letwin, Shirley Robin, vi, xxiv
Lewis, Clive Staples, 5
Liberty Fund, Inc., 133
Lincoln, Abraham, 112
Lipset, Seymour Martin, 87
Lipsett, Don, xix
Liszt, Franz, 150
Livius, Titus, 118
Livy, 118
Locke, John, 44, 113, 115, 126, 171
Louis Philippe, 142, 150
Louis XVI of France, 141
Lowe, Vivian, xix
Lutz, Friedrich A., 111, 126
Lynch, Alberto Benegas, xxiv

MacDonagh, O., 85
Mach, Ernst, 43
Machlup, Fritz, vi, xix, xxiii
Macleod, Henry, 43
Madariaga, Salvador de, 108
Madison, James, 142
Mandeville, Bernard de, 43, 44
Marget, Arthur, 18, 25
Maritain, Jacques, 98
Martino, Antonio, xxiv
Marx, Carl, 72, 80, 149
Mason, Alpheus T., 142
McConnell, Eleanor, xix
Meinecke, Friedrich, 130
Menger, Carl, 43, 44, 68, 173
Meyer, Fritz W., 126
Michelet, Jules, 130
Mill, John Stuart, 43, 109, 148, 149
Milton, John, 149
Mises, Ludwig von, 6, 9, 31, 34, 102, 103, 173
Mitchell, Wesley Clair, 44
*Monetary Nationalism and International Stability*, 174
*Monetary Theory and the Trade Cycle*, 16, 174

180